How About Now?

Satsang with Arjuna

Edited by
**Kate Bishop
and Illona Hanson**

Second Printing
2000

SELF X PRESS

Nevada City, California

How About Now?
Satsang with Arjuna
by Arjuna Nick Ardagh

Published by

Self**X**Press

An imprint of the
Living Essence Foundation
Box 2746 Grass Valley CA 95945
tel: (530) 478-5985
fax:(530) 478-0641
e-mail: orders@livingessence.com
world wide web:http://www.livingessence.com

Printed in the United States of America on acid-free recycled paper using soy-based inks.

ISBN   1-890909-63-7 (pbk.)

Contents

1 The Antidote 1
2 The End of Seeking. 13
3 Value the Diamond 28
4 Relaxing into That. 30
5 Looking Beyond Changing Phenomena . . 31
6 Awareness Itself 34
7 The Real 44
8 Worship Only This 45
9 Relish Risk 46
10 The Window of Eternity 47
11 Cuckoo Banana 49
12 Start at the End. 64
13 The Clue 65
14 The Mutuality of Wakefulness 66
15 Relax Preference 70
16 Give Up the Struggle 71
17 Marriage 73
18 Who Wants to be Enlightened? 74
19 Already Here. 79
20 No Preparation Required 80
21 Wipe the Altar Clean. 86
22 A Natural Response to Life. 87
23 Embrace Everything 91
24 Freedom from the Need to be Free. 92
25 What is in the Way of Finding? 94

26 The Individual is Doomed 95

27 The Wave is Already Wet 96

28 The Mind is a Trickster 97

29 Invisible Secret 99

30 Energy and Consciousness 100

31 Rest Here 102

32 Drop In First 103

33 Listen to the Heart 104

34 It's Different Now 105

35 Nowhere to Go 115

36 In the Fire 116

37 Go Out and Boogie 117

38 Let Go 120

39 We Meet as Beginners 121

40 No Preferences 122

41 Surrender 124

42 The Mirror 127

43 Doubt is a Thought 128

44 Embrace Contradiction 133

45 Surrender All to the Divine Mother 136

46 The Birth of Love 140

47 Embrace Pain 141

48 Seeds of Love 148

49 Heartbreak 154

50 Welcome Everything 156

51 The Pull of the Heart 157

52 Benefits 161

53 Natural Respect 163

54 Only Now 167

55 Your Own Truth 168

Dedication

*This book is dedicated in endless gratitude
to the ones who ripped the veil
Sri Ramana Maharshi
and Sri H.W.L.Poonjaji.*

*And to my sons
Abhi and Shuba.*

Bhagavan Sri Ramana Maharshi (1879-1950)

Sri H.W.L. Poonjaji (1910-1997)

Preface

This book is taken from transcripts of public meetings conducted by Arjuna from Valentine's Day 1998 to Valentine's Day 1999. Arjuna conducts such meetings several times a week, both here in Nevada City where he lives, as well as in a number of other cities in the US and in Europe. The meetings are called "Satsang": gatherings in association with the Truth.

Some of the transcripts remain as dialogs: conversations between Arjuna and the old and new friends who come and talk with him on the couch at the front of the room. Other pieces have become prose: longer discourses that lent themselves to a more thorough exploration of a topic. Some of the transcripts playfully called out to us to be transformed into poetry, and so we obeyed them. You will find these poetic renderings scattered freely throughout the book.

Everything you read here was spoken unrehearsed and in response to whoever was present. We have done our best to clean up the grammar and to remove irrelevant diversions, otherwise the words remain true to the spontaneous and unpredictable dance of Truth with Itself. We hope you will find this book an opportunity to dive deeply into the limitless ocean of your own Living Essence.

Audio and video tapes are available of many of the Satsangs presented here. You are welcome to contact us for more information.

Kate Bishop — editor
Nevada City, California
August 1999.

1

The Antidote

There are a few very simple, undeniable, and basic observations we can make about the state of being human. These are not special or esoteric, they are more in the realm of common sense.

First, we are all in some way or other constantly preoccupied with changing phenomena. Human consciousness is continually tracking something that is changing. Have you noticed? This activity is almost unceasing except at night, when there is relative unconsciousness—sleep. During waking and dreaming hours, consciousness is constantly velcroed to something which is changing.

Relationship is an example. When it is not there, we may be quite happy without it. Then along it comes. Consciousness glues onto it and says, "my relationship," and all may be well for a while. Then, at a certain point, the person either leaves, or dies, or things somehow change, and there is no longer "my relationship." It disappears again, and we suffer. We velcro attention in this way to all kinds of situations, people and things: my finances; my car; my family; my children. In fact "my life" is composed of all the different things which attention has fixated on.

This is the human condition. At a microscopic level, moment to moment, consciousness is fixating on thoughts. First, there is no thought. Then a thought arises and attention glues onto it, and everything else has disappeared. When a thought comes of "my dinner," everything else is gone, and "my dinner" is all that remains. Then the thought disappears, and later we cannot even remember what it was.

The same is true with "my feelings." First, there is nothing there; then anger comes. We don't generally have the experience that "I am experiencing anger." Instead we say, "I am angry now."

The object, which is being seen through the filter of anger, is now completely colored by the anger.

Similarly, feelings in "my body" completely overshadow awareness. We say, "I am sick," or "I am tired," and we identify completely with these feelings.

This is the human condition. I am not aware of anyone who is immune to this, are you? Maybe Sri Sri Sri Banananandaraj claims to be, but I have not actually met anybody who is immune to this changing procession of phenomena. This is our lot as human beings.

The other undeniable thing about being human is that we undergo a fair amount of unnecessary suffering. By this I don't mean the inevitable aches and pains in the body or the unavoidable changing phenomena of life; people die, things shift and change. What I am pointing to is unnecessary suffering, the anguish created by thought that is simply unnecessary. It is difficult to see this in ourselves. We don't think, "Oh, I'm experiencing some unnecessary suffering now." Instead, we say to ourselves, "I've got a raw deal. I'm married to a complete idiot," or "My kids are driving me crazy," or "My job is just not right for me, I don't make enough money and I can't pay the bills." We tell ourselves that it is because of these things that we suffer.

If you look at someone else, say your next-door neighbor or a friend, this is where the unnecessary suffering really shows up. If you look at somebody else who is all churned up, to them it seems like they have a really serious problem, but all you want to say is, "Just relax. If you could just be a little patient and relax; everything is fine." Don't you have that feeling sometimes when you are with your family or friends? It is easy to see the unnecessary struggle in those around us, but it is hard to see it in ourselves.

These are inevitable, undeniable facts about the human condition. There is nothing especially spiritual, enlightened or esoteric about it. This is just a simple fact that consciousness is constantly gluing onto changing events and that we suffer unnecessarily. It is very simple.

There is something else that is so simple and obvious that it misses our attention. If you look around the room where you are sitting, what do you see? Maybe you see curtains, flowers, furniture, or other people. One thing that you would probably not think of noticing is the air in the room. You see the visible things without noticing the air, although the room is actually full of air. This space is full of oxygen and nitrogen, but we don't think about the air. We focus on the objects that fill the room.

There is something similar about human experience that is almost always overlooked. This is not Islam, Hinduism, Buddhism or any kind of "ism," but simple, practical common sense. Once you see the point, the whole house of cards comes tumbling down, and you live in a different universe. This is the good news. It just so happens that this secret was passed onto me by a friend who was Indian, but he could just as well have been French. It doesn't make any difference. This secret is universal to everyone.

All thoughts, all feelings, all physical sensations, all seeming problem states share one thing in common that is almost always overlooked: the nature of the one who is experiencing. In order for there to be a thought, there must be something thoughtless experiencing the thought. That is clear, isn't it? For a thought to be recognized as a thought, there must be something that is not thinking that sees the thought. In order for us to say, "I am having a thought," something other than thought must be recognizing thought.

It is the same when you notice emotion: "Ah, there's anger." Mostly we are so caught up in it we don't even notice the anger, we just see the object through the anger. But once you notice anger, jealousy, fear, anxiety or joy, it becomes obvious that something other than feeling is noticing feelings. You could call that peace. Something peaceful is noticing the stirred-up feelings.

It is the same with the physical body. We notice sensations in the physical body. Obviously, something non-physical, something that has no form is noticing the sensations in the body. This is also common sense. To notice sensations in the body, there must be something disembodied to notice the body, and that is almost always overlooked. Once this is recognized, things are very simple. But when thought comes, we forget all about the thoughtlessness that is noticing the thought. When feelings come, we forget all about the peace noticing the feelings. When the body is being experienced, we forget all about that which is disembodied, noticing the body. For many people who hear this, the question then arises, "So what?"

This is the essence of what I want to share with you, this "So what?" Let us discover why, if this mystery can be embraced and noticed, it can change the whole nature of everything. I am not saying that your life is necessarily going to get better. This is not about self-improvement. Things might improve, but there are no guarantees. There is something much deeper than self-improvement. Most of us in this culture have participated in many kinds of efforts to improve our lives, but the very fact that we have already done so much suggests that something is not working as well as we had hoped. It suggests that there might be something about self-improvement that does not live up to the way it was advertised.

We have tried to change our thoughts, feelings and patterns of behavior in so many ways. We have tried to change negative thoughts into positive ones, undesirable feelings into pleasant ones, and dysfunctional behaviors into productive ones. We put positive affirmations on the refrigerator door or on the mirror. But how well has it worked? How long does it last? How successful are we at changing the habits of this human monkey? Most people discover that we are not always so successful. Let's examine why the question, "Who is experiencing all this?" is so deeply transformative. Although it may not make you a better human monkey, it does awaken you to That which is not a human monkey at all.

When you look at a painting, whether the "Mona Lisa," the "Birth of Venus" or anything you find beautiful, where is the beauty coming from? Where is the source of the beauty? It is obviously not coming out of the painting, or everyone would agree that one painting is beautiful and another is ugly. Obviously, the beauty must be projected from somewhere else onto the painting.

In the same way, think of someone you really love. If you think of that person or see them, you feel an upwelling of love in your heart. But if I saw your favorite person from across the room, would I feel the same love that you do? Unless I know them, it is unlikely. I have two sons, one is four years old and the other is seven. My seven year old is a very intense boy. He has a lot of energy. I love him; he's my son. When I go to school to pick him up, I look across the playground at all the kids, and when my eyes light on him, my heart is aflame with love, because he's my son. But not everybody has that same feeling when they see my seven-year-old son. Where is the source of the love? Where does it come from? It comes from you and is projected onto the object. It must be like that. If the love were coming from my son, everyone would fall in love with him as I do. He would be very happy about that, but that is not the way it is. Love comes from consciousness, from the perceiver, but this is not how we live our lives. We meet someone and act as though they are the source of our love. We say, "Don't leave me. Stay with me! I don't want to lose this love." And then if they try to get away (which they probably will because we're holding on so tightly), we experience abandonment.

There are all kinds of things that we glue onto in this way. We say, "This is the source of my happiness, my security, my love, the source of my well-being." All these things shift and change; they all eventually go away, and we suffer. This may not be clear when you look at your own life, because the attachment is so strong. But when you look at someone else, it is clear that it is the attachment that causes suffering more than the presence or absence of an object. When you look at someone going through a relationship drama, it is obvious that a year before they had the relationship, they were doing fine, probably better than they are now. They became involved in a relationship, things got stirred up, and when the relationship ended they went into suffering. Obviously, the happiness is not coming from the object because they were fine before the drama began.

There is an antidote to all this. When the antidote is applied, it works one hundred percent of the time. I am here only to share this antidote. I travel to different cities to deliver this serum and to celebrate the health that it brings.

The antidote only works when you use it. If you have an illness, you can go to the hospital and the doctor may say, "This is not a big deal; your illness is very simple to cure. You need to take this particular prescription." Then he gives you a piece of paper. But the paper doesn't cure the illness. If you put the prescription in your pocket, nothing will happen. You have to take the piece of paper to the pharmacy, buy a little bottle and read the instructions. When you go home, you pop a pill in your mouth. Then, if the doctor gave you the right medicine, the symptoms will disappear.

It is the same with this antidote. It works only when it is applied. It opens a perspective that is sometimes called an "awakened view." Some people even get really carried away and call it an "enlightened view." I would call it common sense, simple sanity. In comparison, the rest of the way we have led our life looks highly inadvisable.

The simple antidote to everything we have examined here rests in the one simple question, "Who am I? Who is the one experiencing all this?"

This is not a spiritual practice, although one might try to make it into one. It is similar to asking "What is the time?" You ask the question, and you look at your watch to see the answer. Or, "What color is the carpet?" You inquire and look down to determine the answer. To know the answer to any question, it must be treated in this direct way. It is just like that with this question. When you sincerely ask the question, "Who am I?" with the honest intention to find the answer, the antidote to suffering is immediate.

Look back into yourself, right now, and find out what is there. Look back into the experiencer itself, and what do you find?

What is there? What kind of something or nothing do you find when you ask yourself, "Who am I?"

(After some silence, a response from the audience) *Just awareness.*

Okay. Now what is awareness like? What is the nature of awareness?

It's very open. It doesn't have any content.

If you took a tape measure and measured it, how big is it?

It's infinite. It's not in this realm of finiteness at all.

When you look back into awareness itself, when was it created?

It has no beginning or end.

Excellent! It is eternal. It has no beginning and no ending. It is timeless. It is infinite and eternal. And who are you?

I am That.

"I am That" which is infinite and eternal. Now, if you just rest for a moment in that recognition, "I am That," what problem exists in this moment?

No real problem.

No real problem. I love how you say that. We could imagine problems, but if we rest in the silent answer to this question, "Who am I?" we rest as That, which is infinite, eternal, and there is no real problem. And tell me, if we rest as That, which is infinite and eternal, can you actually find anything real here called "the mind?" If you think, you can imagine anything—you immediately make concepts. But if you just stay in

7

that which is infinite and eternal, is there anything real called the mind?

No, there's nothing real.

From this wakefulness, was there ever anything real called the mind?

No.

Is there anything real called ego? If you rest with the answer that comes to that question, is there anything that is a separate entity, separate from consciousness itself?

It appears to be separate.

Yes, it appears to be separate. But is that real or is it the product of thought? If we don't pay attention to thought, is there anything real that is separate?

No.

What this man is saying is the exact same realization that Buddha gave testimony to in his teachings. It is the same realization that Lao Tzu speaks of in the *Tao Te Ching*. It is the same realization that runs throughout Zen and the Dzogchen teachings in Tibetan Buddhism. It is that which Jesus spoke of when he said, "I and my Father are one." What is spoken now is the eternal awakened view. The good news is that anyone, and I mean anyone — not just people who have been seekers or who have bought the right books or done the right practice — anyone now can have this, now, and now, and now. Anyone, anywhere can have this.

This antidote to suffering is just common sense. It happens to have been handed down from Asian traditions because their attention was more on the internal and less on the external and, perhaps, now they have their own set of problems as a result. There are many aspects of economic life that don't work very well in the material realm in Eastern countries because their attention was on another dimension. Now we have a little cross-fertilization going into effect. They are learning about computer technology at the moment, and we have something to gain from their traditions that have focused on the eternal. Computers are not intrinsically American; a computer works just as well in India as it does in America. If an Indian were to say to you, "I don't know if I want to use your computer; it's American, and I'm Indian," you could explain to him, "No, the computer is just a computer. You can use it anywhere. It doesn't have to be used only in America." Similarly, this antidote, although it has been more prevalent in the Orient, is simply common sense. It applies anywhere.

What we are speaking of here applies to all six billion people on this planet. This is very, very good news. In the 1960's there began a thirst in this country for something more substantial than met the eye. We reflected on our parents and their culture and, to many of us, something didn't feel right. We began importing teachers from other cultures, thinking to ourselves, "Well, our politicians obviously don't know what's going on, and neither do our religious leaders or parents, so let's import something new. Maybe other cultures will have a better understanding of what is meaningful in life." We imported Indians, Tibetans, Chinese, anyone who was as different as possible from what was familiar to us, and sadly, with whom we were also eventually disillusioned.

We agreed that they were the enlightened ones because they spoke from this view. Mostly they had long beards, long robes, long unpronounceable names and — once they were established in this country — long stretch limousines. We became accustomed to this model of enlightenment. The Holy One would sit on the throne and speak from this view, and we would sit on the floor and say, "That is enlightenment up there. I am only a lesser mortal, working on my issues, and maybe one day I'll be like that too." Many of those teachers kept saying to us, "No, no. You are also That!" We would think, "Ultimately, I guess it may be true and, when I'm enlightened later, it will be true. But right now I am struggling, and I had better listen to the Holy One on the throne."

During the 1970's most of those teachers established large organizations, and by the 1980's many of those organizations had become somewhat corrupt. This is not to point the finger here or there at a particular teacher, but we are all human. No one can hold a projection perfectly. We put these poor people into such elevated positions. We projected so many fantasies onto them. One was preaching celibacy and, meanwhile, he was having fun in the back room with a teenager. Another was preaching renunciation, while amassing a large Swiss bank account. And another was preaching the renunciation of power, while building a large hierarchical organization. What could we expect? During the 1980's many of these teachers were exposed to be other than what we had dreamed of, and we were disappointed. I would not put the responsibility only on the teachers. We were all projecting like crazy.

There is good news now. We don't have to do that anymore. Along with the holes in the ozone layer, large holes have begun to appear in the collective veil of separation. In the 1960's, when these teachers first arrived, there was no way for us to have direct realization. It was next to impossible. You could listen to the right words and repeat them verbatim, but it was not possible until a few years ago to sit firmly in the realization that "I am awareness, infinite and eternal." Such realizations were not happening for ordinary Westerners, or at most very fleetingly. The consciousness began to shift in our culture in this decade, in the 1990's. Now, if we seek out teachings of awakening, they are mostly being shared by ordinary Westerners — people just like you and me. There are very few Indian teachers left. These days, spiritual teachers of note — Byron Katie, Catherine Ingram, Isaac Shapiro, Hanuman, Satyam Nadeen — are all Western people. There is a new generation now, and it is all up to us. The good news is that if this shift from the identification with form to being formlessness itself can happen to an ordinary Western person with children, a bank balance and the rest of it, it can happen to you, too. There is really no reason left for anyone to be a seeker. Right here, tonight, you can take off your Seeker Badge. I don't recommend putting a Finder Badge in its place because that is just another form of identification. You can be awareness, consciousness itself. This is profoundly good news.

Let's be very truthful and honest with each other. Just like anyone who teaches the eternal truth, I am sitting here in a somewhat dangerous position. This seat has potential for great projection. That is nobody's fault; it's just the theater of the situation that invites a certain amount of projection. So let me come clean. I have been asked by my teacher, who in turn was asked by his teacher, to pass on this good news. I sit here as a messenger of That which is available to you right now. But in every other regard I am exactly like you. You could come up with the most extreme reason why you think that you can't have this awakening right now: "Well, I get irritated with my kids." So do I. "Well, I get anxious about my financial situation." So do I. "Well, when I haven't had enough sleep, I get grouchy." So do I.

None of this is as it seems to the mind. It has nothing to do with changing anything at all. There is nothing wrong with trying to improve things. In fact, it becomes easier to make improvements once you disidentify from being what you are trying to change. If you yell at your kids, although it is probably better that you do not yell, that has nothing to do with realization. The personality can be fairly neurotic and still this realization is absolutely available to you. This is great news. You can have freedom now, just as you are. It doesn't matter at all what is happening in your life. It doesn't matter what your personality is like. None of that matters. There is a way that whatever is happening in your life, including the worst, can become an invitation to go even deeper into wakefulness. Suffering is probably the best way to reach depths of understanding. Suffering cuts attachment. This is profoundly good news. This is the time right now, at the end of the millennium, when there can be widespread awakening.

I travel to many cities in the U.S. and Europe and everywhere people are having the same experience. In the beginning people doubt it because it seems elementary, so ordinary that they can't believe it could be so simple. But it is this very simplicity that allows you to rest as the source of love, as the source of everything for which you have been grasping.

Every kind of fulfillment you have tried to find in your ordinary life is available to you in its purity in this very moment right now, right here. Experiment for yourself. There is absolutely no reason to take anything that is said here on faith. This is an entirely scientific inquiry. I recommend that you let yourself be satisfied only with that which completely matches your experience.

2

The End of Seeking

*Y*ou *say that nothing happens, and all it takes is this second. Then why isn't it happening this second to me and everybody in this room? Why are people spending hours with you, or two days, if it really is true that nothing happens and all you need is the longing? Why isn't it spontaneous?*

Because of accumulated concepts.

Why can't the accumulated concepts just be released in a second?

They can.

Why aren't they?

Why aren't they? Because they are being clung to.

Why can't they be released right now?

They can. You want to uncling right now?

Yes.

Come up here. But beware, I mean business!

(She walks up to the raised podium)

What is it you really want, sitting here. Do you really want to be finished with seeking?

Yes.

Could you let that be stronger than the need to be right?

My mind goes blank when you ask these questions.

That doesn't matter. Just answer from your heart. Could you let the longing to be finished with seeking be stronger than the need to be right about anything?

Yes.

So, as you sit here, with a new face in front of you, a new person, just keep the eyes as they are. That's right. (Incidentally, just for your reference, you are completely ripe. You are dropping from the tree already. You just need to be blown upon.) So just now, sitting here, seeing this form, noticing what's occurring — who is noticing these things? Just look back into yourself and find out, "Who am I?"

I go blank.

Very good. Just stay there with "I go blank." When you ask yourself, "Who am I?" what is found?

Nothing.

Nothing, okay. Now just rest as this. From here, was there ever anything that answered to that question?

No.

No, okay. Now could you just relax a little more into what has been seen? Could you just relax for a moment into the actuality that there is nothing there called "I?" Could you, just for a moment, relax into the recognition that there is nobody experiencing this?

I can't believe that.

It doesn't matter. You don't need to believe it. It has been seen, hasn't it? You have asked, "Who am I?" and nothing was found. Now just for a moment, could you just savor the inevitability of it?

Nothing changes. I'm looking for something to feel different.

Exactly. What did Buddha say? "Nothing happened to me under the *bodhi* tree." Waiting for something to happen is what you have been doing all your life. Do you understand? Your entire life you have been waiting for an experience, and this is called seeking.

Now tell me, could you just for a moment stop waiting for something to happen?

I don't know.

I'm not asking you to do it. I'm just asking theoretically; could you just put aside the habit of waiting? Is it possible to put that aside for a moment?

My mind goes so blank when I...

Exactly! Of course it goes blank. Could you relax into blankness? Blankness is where it's at! Just be blank for a moment. You see, you're waiting for a fireworks display, which is just another experience. When you get down to the nitty gritty, you are left with no experience at all, and it's unfamiliar. It is not what the mind is expecting. The mind has an entire fabrication set up about enlightenment.

Well, "freedom," it sounds pretty good. This "nothing" doesn't feel like that.

How About Now?

Be a little patient! We can go much deeper.

We're not there yet? So that's another experience.

No. We're here. But we may not have relaxed fully into here yet, do you see? For instance, we're in Fairfield, Iowa, right? But as long as we're still craving Paris, we haven't quite relaxed into being in Fairfield. It is as though you have been journeying and journeying and you finally arrive in Fairfield. You park the car, but you are so much in the habit of journeying that it takes a moment to relax and realize, "We have arrived!"

Well, this is it?

This has always been it.

Yes, but this can't be it. It's nothing.

That's right, it's nothing!

But so what?!

Exactly! That is the point! So what? Why make such a big deal about something so simple?

But if my body were in the midst of severe pain right now, I know that this wouldn't do it. I think I would still be extraordinarily attached and that I would be thinking, "So what. I'm not experiencing freedom in this." Do you know what I mean?

Yes, I understand. Yet the one thing I can tell you is that when you touch into that blankness, if you could savor it for what it is, it would give you what you want. You discard it right away because you are more interested in having experiences. You overlook what is hidden in the blankness.

What you are passing through is what everyone passes through. Something is happening for you because I can see it in your eyes. Something is beginning to take you over. So just hang in there, okay? You may say this is nothing, but I wonder why your eyes are so shiny all of a sudden!

Everything is up to valuing. If you are addicted to having more experiences, more change, more ways to make life comfortable, then you are going to trip across freedom and overlook it completely. You are too addicted to this realm and trying to make life better. Immediately you say, "Well, if I were in pain, this wouldn't help me alleviate the pain." This is not medicine. This is freedom.

Nisargadatta Maharaj, one of the greatest teachers of this century, was once asked, "In what way will realization benefit my life materially?" And he replied, "In no way whatsoever. If you are trying to attain self-improvement from this, forget all about it."

I don't want self-improvement. I want to feel better, to feel more happiness, freedom, joy, love. Doesn't everybody? Isn't that normal?

That is normal, and that's called being hooked into *samsara* (the continual flow of desires). What will result from chasing more joy and more happiness? You will experience suffering because they go together. Chasing after happiness and joy and all these things only brings you more and more suffering because of your attachment to them. At a certain point, you begin to realize that it is all a trick. It's called *samsara*; it's called *maya* (illusion). Then you're ready to find out, "Who Am I?" Ask it now. Are you ready to give up the pursuit of happiness, of pleasure and the acquisition of the imaginary truth?

The funny thing is, you'll get it all back again with interest. But you can't do it for that reason. You will get everything you want, but for now you have to choose freedom and only freedom.

When I met my teacher, Poonjaji, I told him with absolute sincerity, not poetically, "I am ready to die if that is what is required. I am perfectly willing for this body to die. There is no hesitation in me." And it was true. I was completely ready to give up everything.

I'm too scared.

That is honest. But again, at least now, ask yourself, "Who am I?" Just ask it. Who is aware here? Who is present? Just ask that. Really ask, "Who is aware of all this occurring?"

(There is no answer)

Ah, there is silence. This word, "I," what does it refer to? You see, you can take the word, "jacket," and it has an object that goes with it—name and form, you see? You can take the word, "watch," a five-letter word, which is a symbol for an object. Now this word, "I," find the object that belongs with it. There is nothing like that. Just stay with this for a little bit. There is nothing like "I," is that true? And yet this moment is being experienced. It is not being experienced by an "I" or "me" because there is nothing like that which exists. So what experiences this moment?

I don't know.

But it is being experienced, isn't it? This is definitely being experienced.

It feels like some individual something.

Then look for it. Look for the individual something; just seek it out.

It can't be found, but that does not mean it's not there.

In eight years of teaching in this way, full time every day, no one has ever, ever been able to find it. Why not?

*But something has to be experiencing this, or we wouldn't be here.
There is something that is me, and there is something that is you. There
is something.*

That's what you have been told. Just stay with what can actually be verified. Can you find a thing called "I?" There is a body,
but can you find this individualized consciousness?
Can you find it?

No.

Yet this is being experienced. All this is just common sense,
isn't it? You can't find an "I." I have worked with thousands of
people. Not one of them has been able to find the thing they call
"I," not once. I watched Poonjaji work with thousands of people.
Now I am not saying that everybody rests in emptiness when
they can't find the "I." A lot of people just recreate the concept
again. It is up to you.

I don't want to do that.

Then don't do it.

How?

Start hitting your knee with your hand.

(She pats her knee)

Do it hard, harder.

(She hits her knee harder)

Now stop.
You see, you stopped. You just stopped because hitting your
knee is a silly thing to do. How are you going to stop imagining

something that is not there? Just stop. You stop because it's ridiculous to keep recreating something that does not exist. It doesn't serve any purpose. It just creates unnecessary suffering. If you want to suffer some more, if you want to continue chasing after desire, then that's your brand of freedom. It is your option. But if you choose to rest in this recognition, you are also welcome. Right now, like it or not, it is being rested in.

Yes.

Thank you at least for acknowledging that. Right now there is resting. Now just stay here for a moment and answer one more thing. In this moment there is nothing, right? Is there any problem now?

No.

Is there anything that needs to be attained now? Could you just rest? There is nothing to hang onto anyway. Now tell me, resting as this, just answer one simple question from your heart, not from concept. Who are you actually meeting here? Not the form, but who is looking back at you now? Answer this from your heart.

Clearly me.

Shout it out!

Clearly me!

This is the truth. It is not poetry. It is not hallucination. You are literally sitting here with your Self. Now look around for a moment; look at the eyes and see who is here in the room.
How many are there in this room?

I know the answer, but I go blank.

So come back here. Who are you meeting here? Slowly, if you can put this on your altar instead of the bric-a-brac you have had there—including all your seeking and your many practices—if you can put this emptiness on your altar, slowly you will see "me" everywhere. By "me" I mean this "Me" that is everyone.

You go to the market. Look into the eyes of the person who is checking out your groceries. "There I am again!" It is all you everywhere, and it is not just philosophy. It is actually true. Now tell me one thing now. In this moment here, is there anything real called "ego?"

You want the truth?

Yes, I want to know if you can find it, not think about it.

I think I can think of it.

Yes, you can think of elephants dancing in pink under-wear. It doesn't mean they are here. You can think of any-thing. Anything can be created in thought. Is there something real here called "ego?"

No.

Was there ever anything real called "ego?"

In those moments of its absence, no.

Even in the moments when it appears to exist, is there actu-ally something called "ego" or is there an imagining of it?

Imagining.

Do you understand that? It is imagination. The entire spiritual path is all imagination. It is the imagining of some-thing called "ego" that then has to be removed. What a struggle to work so hard to banish something that is not there! This is a waste of time. All spiritual seeking is a waste of time. It is a waste of life.

Could you just rest here now? Could you burn all the concepts that you have been fed? You don't have to do it. I am just asking, could you?

Yes.

Will you? What would be the advantage of going back to imagining all kinds of trouble and having to get rid of it?

I'm just afraid that the habit would come back. It is so strong.

The invitation is available.
Is there anything real in this moment called "mind?" Can you find something called "mind?"

I can find something that operates a lot.

You find thoughts. Can you find a thing called "mind?"

No.

These thoughts that arise, do they interfere with being what you are?

They don't, but it feels like they do.

What is the actuality?

They don't.

The invitation is here to remain as This. You have a choice to give your allegiance to "I can't do this" and then, of course, that becomes true. But know that there is also the invitation just to put

that thought aside and realize there is nobody who has to do anything. This is the truth.

Do you want to try something really outrageous? Tell them
(points to the others in the room) who you really are. Because this is
what it takes, you see. I spent a year living with Poonjaji. The
realization was perfectly intact, but there was still a wobbling.
Then he said, "Go and teach. Go to the West and spread this as
much as you can." I thought he was asking me to go and help
other people. But he was telling me to teach for me because that
is how it becomes stable.

Tell them now, tell them who you really are.

I feel terrified.

Then all the more reason to do it. "Screw your courage to the
sticking place," as Lady Macbeth said. Sooner or later you will
have to do it. Sooner or later you will have to come out of the
closet if you want to live this. Sooner or later you will have to
meet the world as one no longer seeking. Why not now?

*I guess I don't believe it. I don't personally believe it. I go in and out
so much.*

I understand. If you listen to thought at all, it is going to inval-
idate everything.

Do you understand why? Because this realization basically
is the death of the thought machine. Thought screams out,
"Don't listen to that guy. He's dangerous. He's a charlatan."
Because if you listen to this guy, thought no longer will have
rule in your kingdom. Every single thought is revealed to be a
lie, every one. You can live your life perfectly well without
thinking at all.

Really?

Absolutely. In fact things go much better.

How About Now?

What a relief!

I want to qualify that for a moment so there is just truth spoken here. The living of this is not instantaneous. The realization is easy. Every single human being on this planet, in order to remain in a body, somehow has a foot in both camps.

So what is different?

The abandonment of seeking, that's all. The content does not necessarily change. Thoughts arise, and feelings come and go. But there is no longer this concept, "I should be different." It is from here that peace arises. It is not the way you thought it was. Essentially, you were waiting to escape from being human. I suggest you embrace being human. Enjoy being human.

Just now, you see? Just now you are at peace. You are perfectly at peace. There is nothing wrong in this moment, is there? Is there any problem if a thought comes? Does it matter if a thought passes through?

Truthfully, they feel annoying. It's more peaceful to not have all these thoughts of, "What about this, and what about that?"

Yes, but could you just let them pass? Let me ask you, before the thoughts arise, do you decide to have them?

No.

They just appear anyway, right?

Yes.

So they are out of control. What difference does it make if you fight them or not? Could you just let them pass?

Yes.

Now could you just say to them, "You are welcome?" Just tear down the barbed-wire fence and say, "Come and play in my garden."

Yes.

Now does it make any difference to peace?

No!

How about emotions? Could they come and go?

Oh, God! I really don't like some of them.

I know. And does it serve you to not like them?

No, it doesn't really.

Don't they come on their own?

They really do.

If you lock your door and barricade yourself against them, what do they end up doing?

They show up anyway and pound the door down.

They pound the door down or they get in through the window, right? So why not just open the door and welcome them in? And I will tell you one thing, if you open your doors and welcome them as guests, you will find that each and every one of them is a friend with a gift. I can tell you this from personal experience.

Unbearable as it may seem, once you open the door and say, "Come in and sit by the fire," grief becomes your depth. Jealousy

will become your freedom. Anger will become your power.
Welcome everything.

Tell me now, what can disturb peace now?

Pain.

Could you even welcome pain in the name of freedom? If it
meant your freedom, could you welcome pain? You think that
awakening is the end of pain? Actually, it is the end of identification, but everything that has been pushed away rushes in to be
completed.

If you welcome pain, if you just say to it, "Come," it will not
disturb peace. It will just pass through like a guest. So in the name
of this freedom which you are now resting in, could you include
pain, too? If you just try it, you will find there is nothing to resist.

When we began our conversation this evening, you said,
*"Well, if accumulated concepts can be let go of in a second, what is the point
in spending time here?"* Do you see that in sitting here, we have
dissolved a lot of false concepts?

Yes.

Can you see that it was only those concepts that prevented the
peace?

Yes.

They are only concepts. They are only false ideas. Do you see
now why one needs a little time?

Thank you.

There is no reason to leave this if you can just abandon the
allegiance to the idea, "I can't do it." There is no "I," and there is
nothing to do. Truly, the invitation is to rest here. Even in the
midst of trouble, there is rest.

Any problem now?

No.

And now?

No.

That's all. You've got it. All there is, is now.

You know what? I'll tell you something. I have a nose for these things. The thoughts might say, "This could go away." But I'll tell you what I can smell. It's going to get deeper, and deeper, and deeper. It's going to take over your heart in such depth of love and compassion that you will drown in it ecstatically. And there is nothing you can do about it!

The gates are wide open, you see. You can choose to hang on to cynicism, to tradition, to ideas and teachings, but what does it give you? Or, you can choose freedom now. You can choose to be That. It is available right now, and now, and now. It is not a state of being that you access by flipping a switch, and after that you are enlightened.

It is a choice that is made every single moment of every day — to choose freedom over the soap opera.

3

Value the Diamond

There was once in India a dobhi-wallah (a man who does laundry). He lived in a town atop a little mountain, and below in the valley was a stream. Every day he would collect all the laundry from the people in the village, take his old donkey down to the stream and wash the sheets and other laundry in the stream. Then he would put the laundry back in the baskets and go all the way up to the town again. His donkey was very old, very weary, and close to collapse. One day he was walking down to the stream and caught sight of a bright, shiny object in the bushes. He picked it up and exclaimed, "Oh, how beautiful!" He put the object on a string and placed it around his donkey's neck like a medallion.

A few days later, a diamond merchant came to that city to do business. As he walked down the hill at the end of the day, the dobhi-wallah was walking up—and they met. The diamond merchant took one look at the dobhi-wallah and the donkey, and said, "My God! I'll give you 50,000 rupees for that!" The dobhi-wallah's mouth dropped open, and he thought to himself, "This guy must be mad! My donkey is about to die, and he wants to pay me 50,000 rupees!" So gladly he gave the diamond merchant the donkey. The merchant counted out some money and gave the dobhi-wallah enough to retire for the rest of his life.

Then a very strange thing happened. The diamond merchant walked off about four paces, pulled the shiny object off the donkey's neck, left the donkey behind, and walked away. Now the dobhi-wallah was really confused. He said to himself, "This man paid me 50,000 rupees for my donkey, and then he leaves my donkey behind!" The dobhi-wallah was very happy with 50,000 rupees and now also his donkey. The diamond merchant was also happy because he had just purchased for a song the most valuable diamond he had ever seen.

That bright, shiny object has different values according to how it is perceived. If you see it for what it is, the shiny object has intrinsically the capacity to liberate you from trouble forever. That bright shiny object has the capacity to end suffering, but you have to know how to value it. This is the key.

If you take a casual attitude to the Truth, you will have a casual result—pure and simple. You will walk away with some interesting concepts, perhaps a nice experience, but nothing of fundamental nourishment. If you value what is pointed to so supremely that it's as though your hair were on fire, then you are liberated from the identification with, and attachment to, all suffering.

4

Relaxing Into That

And simply in the returning
To That which does not change,

There is,
Like a fish slipping into water,

A relaxing into Something

Which one recognizes
Always to have been.

5

Looking Beyond Changing Phenomena

As human beings
We are generally caught in a spin
Of changing phenomena—
Thoughts which arise,
Spin around for a while
And then disappear—
Emotional atmospheres which color our reality,
And then change the next day.
We are preoccupied with physical sensations
And conditions of the body
That come and then change.
We become preoccupied with problems
That seem to need action,
That demand solutions.
We become preoccupied with relationships
That seem to be,
At least temporarily,
The only source of happiness for us.
"If only I could stay with this person,
Everything would be okay."
Or, "If only I could get away from this person
Everything would be okay."
Human consciousness
Is preoccupied with phenomena;
Things that come,
Perpetuate for awhile,
And then disappear.

HOW ABOUT NOW?

It is hard to think
Of any human being
Who is not somehow caught
In the desire to have this
Or to get rid of that.

There is something
That is almost always overlooked.
The purpose of this gathering here
Is to turn the attention to That
Which has been overlooked.

When we go to a movie theater,
We see flickering images on the screen.
Clark Gable is about to tell Vivian Lee
That he loves her.
We are preoccupied
With these flickering images.
Actually, for most of the movie,
We forget that it's a white screen
With images flickering.
We get caught in the illusion
Of a story happening.
In order for the images to have their allure,
To be convincing,
There must be a white screen.
The screen is empty.
It is capable of reflecting anything
And yet it has no content of its own.
This white screen is generally overlooked.

The very bright bulb behind the film
Is actually the source of all the images.
For each one of those pictures to be there,
There must be a bright bulb.
But in the movie theater

We never think of the bulb,
We only think of the images.
In order for all these phenomena
To be experienced,
In order for all these experiences
To be happening,
There must be something
Other than the experiences
To experience them.
In order for a thought
To be recognized as thought,
There must be something silent,
Not-thought,
Recognizing thought.
In order for emotional atmospheres
To shift and change,
There must be something
Completely unemotional,
Recognizing emotion, experiencing emotion.
In order for the sensations in the physical body
To be recognized and experienced,
There must be something non-physical,
Not-in-form,
To recognize form.
That has been overlooked.
It is for That which we are here today.

6

Awareness Itself

Why do we have a personality or a persona?

I'm not very good with the question why, but we can still explore what is true. Just now, here in this meeting between you and me, things are being perceived, aren't they? This Arjuna form is being perceived and words are being heard. All that is being experienced, isn't it?

Yes.

Now see if you can stay with what is absolutely pure and subjective; see if you can stay true to your experience rather than to anything you've heard. Do you understand the difference?

Yes.

If you stay absolutely true to what is innocent and authentic for you in this moment, who is experiencing this occurring? Look back in yourself and see what is found.

I just feel energy.

You just feel energy moving in the body. That energy, is it being experienced or not being experienced? Is the energy being noticed?

Yes.

Good. Who is noticing it?

Awareness.

Ah, Awareness! Beautiful. Awareness. Now tell me about Awareness itself. What is Awareness like?

It's being.

And if you could take a tape measure to it, where does it end?

Well, it's always only beginning.

(Laughter)

As far as you go, you're still at the beginning, right? This is beautiful. It's always only beginning. And when was the creation date of this Awareness?

(She shakes her head with laughter)

Can it be destroyed? Is there anything that could destroy Awareness itself?

No, because it would just be aware of the destruction.

This Awareness has no limits, does it? No beginning and no end. It's like the sky. It's limitless.
    Now tell me, are you the Awareness noticing form, or are you form experiencing Awareness? Which is true?

I feel the former.

You feel the former. Well shout it out, then! What is it you want to tell me? "I feel," you said, "the former." So what's that, then?

I am the Awareness experiencing everything, the body and the energy in the body.

Shout it out for everyone to hear!

(Laughter) I am Awareness experiencing form! Wow! That sounds great!

What a relief. I am Awareness experiencing form! Now you tell me, from here, is there anything real called personality that you could find right now?

I can't feel it right now.

And how about now?

No.

And how about now?

(She shakes her head)

So tell me, is there anything real that exists called personality? By that I mean, is there anything real, as opposed to that which is imaginary?

Just rest as this Awareness experiencing form. Look and see. Is there actually anything that is real to be found called personality?

You know, when I was meditating, I just felt that it was something that was on the front of me and I just wanted to reach through it.

Give it to me.

Don't you think I need it?

This thing that's on the front of you—give it to me.

(Laughter—she mimes handing him something) Have some more.

I don't see anything. My hand is empty. So tell me, this thing—is it real or imaginary?

I guess it's imaginary. But when I look in the mirror, there's someone there.

There's a nose and two eyes and some hair and some hands. But can you actually directly experience something called personality?

The only way I experience it is through observing it. And I notice that the same sorts of things seem to come up.

Now to experience the same sorts of things coming up—how do you do that? Right now, in this moment here, how do you experience the same sorts of things coming up?

I think about it.

That's right, it's in thought, isn't it? Let's do a little experiment. I want to show you for a moment the difference between what's real and what's imaginary because there are different methods required to rid yourself of what's real and what's imaginary, okay?

Here is a cassette case. Is this real?

It's physically manifested.

In ordinary language, it's real, isn't it?

Right.

To get rid of this, what would we need to do?

Smash it!

How About Now?

Violent, aren't we! Okay, that would be one way. And this wrist-watch here, is it real? Just in ordinary language, is this a real watch?

Yes.

What would you have to do to get rid of that?

We'd have to grind it up to make it disappear.

And how about this cushion? What would we have to do to get rid of that?

Just throw it away.

Do you see this watermelon here? Is this real? *(He mimes holding up a watermelon)*

No. But we could imagine it to be real.

But is it actually real? In ordinary language, is this a real watermelon?

No. It's not actually here.

So this watermelon is just a thought.

Do you have to think or imagine to see the cushion?

No.

Do you have to think or imagine to see the watermelon?

Yes.

So you understand the difference between what is real and what is imaginary?

Yes.

How do you get rid of the watermelon?

Let go of the thought.

Beautiful. You see, to get rid of that which is not real, you simply stop imagining and that's all. Okay? Now with the cassette case, or the watch, or the cushion, it's different. You would have to do something to get rid of them. To get rid of the watermelon, you simply stop imagining it. This is a very important distinction because here is where most spiritual practices lead people astray. They spend decades in very frustrating spiritual practice trying to erode something that was never there in the first place.

Tell me just now—if you don't go into thought, obviously you haven't got a watermelon—so if you don't go into thought, is there anything real now called personality?

No.

How are you going to get rid of it?

Let it go.

Yes, just stop imagining it.

But don't you think I need it at all?

Who? Does who need it?

Awareness?

Just now, it's not a question of whether you need it or not. Does it exist?

How About Now?

Ohhh! (She begins to laugh)

How do I get rid of this watermelon?
Just pretend it's not there and it's already not there.

You don't have to pretend; you just wake up and see.

You just let go of the thought.

So is there any need to keep the watermelon? Does it serve any function?

Not really.

So let's just experiment right now. Tell me who you are again?

Nothing.

But yet this is all happening fine, isn't it? This is happening just fine without pretending to be somebody.

I can be here with you and I don't have to be thinking about who I am, or who I should be, or how I should be speaking, or what I should look like, or who I should be portraying.

Yes. And what's left if you don't do all that?

Awareness.

And how is it to be here?

It's real.

It's real, isn't it? And it's delicious!
Now let me show you one more little beautiful secret, which makes all of life absolutely different. Look now, not at this form,

but through the form into whatever is looking back at you. And what is looking at you now?

My first thought was the same, and my second thought was nothing.

So you look that way back into yourself and what do you find?

I feel like it's just a circle.

Beautiful. So if you look back into your own Self, what's that?

It's just going back through you.

Any difference between what's that way and what's this way?

No. The only difference would be if I were over there and you were over here.

Yes, but just now, look back into your own Self and check again. Look back all the way into your own Self. What's that? Relax back into your Self like falling into a feather bed — and what's there?

I just feel emptiness.

Emptiness — beautiful. Emptiness. Now look this way and what do you recognize as you look all the way through this form? What's looking from this side? What word can you put on that?

There's nothing.

There's nothing. So what's the difference between emptiness and nothing?

Nothing.

So who are you meeting here?

It is my Self.

You're meeting your Self — not in a poetic way. This is not just poetry or mysticism or philosophy. *Weerly and twooly*, scientifically, you are meeting your own Self. You have twenty fingers, four knees, four eyes, two noses — and there's only one of you here. Check around as you go about your day and instead of seeing people as a function, look into their eyes and see who's looking back — and you'll find your Self everywhere. This then, is true compassion. Not fabricated, learned compassion, but true compassionçto see your own Self everywhere.

The good news is that you never have to pick up that idea of being separate again. There's no obligation. You're twenty-one, aren't you? You could live another sixty years and never have to pick up the idea of being separate again. Life will not *just* continue. It will blossom and flourish so much better than with this fictitious watermelon messing everything up all the time.

Right — that I would have to take care of and do something with.

Beautiful! Now look around the room for a minute and let them see these eyes. These are the eyes of Buddha. We hear stories of Buddha and of many different saints; and in this moment, what is shining through this form are the eyes of the Divine.

What do you feel as you look at yourself in all these forms?

Happy!

Beautiful! You see, you look over there *(pointing to her sister and father)*, and you discover your father only ever had one child — and in fact he gave birth to himself.

It's too simple to understand. You can understand the personality and you can understand the complexities. But this is too simple to understand. Just enjoy it, live it. And you're going to, I can see. You have no idea what an incredible contribution and service you can make to so many people just from living this.

Beautiful! You have no idea how many people will naturally be touched just from you resting as this. It's all you that you're touching, of course. This is really the way to alleviate suffering on this planet.

I can be born over and over again!

Yes! That's exactly right. It's always fresh. Enlightenment is not a state, you see. It's a constant invitation. Now, now, now, now! Just to drop what was not there in the first place, to drop imagination and relax, become very soft and relaxed to what is already here. This is a wine to be savored, so precious.

You know I have my bookshelves lined with testimonies to what you are experiencing now. The people in these books are revered as mystics and saints and unusual human beings, but what you're experiencing tonight is no different from what any of them have spoken of. I could read to you Padmasambhava, the founder of Tibetan Buddhism, and what he said is no different from what you are saying tonight. This is Home.

Thank you!

7

The Real

There is a calling to recognize,
Perhaps just for a moment,
The difference between what is real and what is imaginary;
To recognize that there has been an addiction to the imaginary.

Bring your attention to this moment with compassion,
Just long enough that Attention falls in love with This Moment.

This past that has been haunting you is a thought;
This future you are worrying about is not real.
It is thought that will never occur.

Now relax.
Welcome these thoughts,
So that they make no difference.

Come with a longing in your heart for a deeper recognition.

8

Worship Only This

In order for emotional atmospheres to shift and change,
There must be something completely unemotional,
Which recognizes emotion,
Experiences emotion.

In order for sensations in the physical body
To be recognized and experienced,
There must be something non-physical,
Not in form
To recognize form.

Worship only This.

9

Relish Risk

Heart demands the infusion of awakening into ordinary life,
So that one's freedom is no longer conditioned upon a particular
fate.

Relish risk!
Here is the secret ground
For breaking down more and more boundaries.

Let the play of this freedom become increasingly dangerous.

10

The Window of Eternity

Through a simple shift of attention
From object to experiencer,
From phenomena to experiencer of phenomena,
One's perspective can change diametrically.
The birth of this shift occurs with the question,
"Who am I?"
This is not about a future state of enlightenment,
Or something that is going to come to you
If you are really good and work very hard.
This is about what is already here and now.

For words to be heard,
There must be silence
In which the words are occurring.
For form to be recognized,
There must be limitlessness
In which the forms can exist.
For there to be phenomena in time —
Beginning, duration and ending —
There must be an eternity
In which time is occurring.
When you truly understand this,
It will change your life.
Then it becomes obvious.
To perceive anything with limits,
There must be limitlessness
In which it is occurring.
If a phenomenon is taking place
Within something else with bigger limits,

How About Now?

Within what would it be occurring?
This question,
"Who am I?"
Brings one immediately to limitlessness,
To eternity,
To That which is unborn, undying,
To That which has no fear of erasure
And to That which is not separate.
As soon as you look back into your Self
And recognize that there is no separate entity to be found,
Only spaciousness,
Then it is not much of a leap
To look into the eyes of what you thought was another person —
Not at the other person
But through the window of those eyes —
And see the eternity that is common to both of you.
Then what is the difference between
Vast spaciousness and immense boundlessness?
Where does infinity end and eternity begin?
This simple yet profound recognition
Signals the end of separation.

At different times this understanding
Has been given a diversity of exclusive names —
Enlightenment, liberation, Self-realization.
People have spoken of this
In a very exalted way,
With massive amounts of worship,
And fast cars and real estate acquired
In the name of this uncomplicated principle.
It is a simple thing we are speaking of here.
This is everyone's birthright.

11

Cuckoo Banana

I want to stay identified with the Self, and I think I've finally become tired of my mind and my ego and all that.

Gosh, well there's lots of fodder for conversation here, isn't there?

Yeah.

(Laughter)

I should have made notes. I could fill the whole two hours with that much! Okay, so let's go slowly. I want to stay identified...

With truth.

I want to stay with truth. With the Self.

With my Self.

With my Self. Okay, good.
Now, would you rather want it, or have it?

I'd rather have it.

Okay, could you give up the wanting, then?

Whatever it takes.

Okay. *(snaps his fingers)*   Like that, you see. Now what's left? Now you've given up wanting your Self, what remains?

Well, there's something there.

Something there. What is that?

I guess it's the Self.

Ohhh! I see. *(laughter)*   Well, what flavor is it?

I don't know that it has a flavor, but it feels blissful and comforting.

So, what remains now?

Well, I'm not sure.

You see, if someone is wanting, wanting, wanting to be in California—"I want to be in California more than anything else, I want to be in California"—where do you suppose they might be?

Some place other than California.

Must be. They've got to be in Kentucky, or Virginia, or New York, or England. "I want to be in California!!!" If someone is sitting in San Francisco saying, "I want to be in California" then what kind of a situation do we have?

A confusion of some sort.

(Laughter)

Well, that's a polite word for it. A little bit cuckoo banana, I'd say. *(Laughter)* Sitting in California and wanting to be in California, this is a case of, to use clinical psychological language, cuckoo banana, you see.

That's me, I guess.

Okay, so who are you?

Most of the time I'm that, anyway.

No, not most of the time. What is "most of the time," now?

Well, most of the time I'm caught up in my mind.

Where is "most of the time" now? What is "most of the time?"

At work...

Yeah, where is "work" now. What is that?

That's where I go to earn money...

Where is "money," "work," "most of the time?" Where are all these things? I only see people sitting in the room.

Well...

Be very accurate. Where is "most of the time I'm caught up?" Where is that, now? Stay very present. Where is "most of the time?"

I don't experience it right now.

Exactly, you see. "Most of the time" is a thought.

Right.

Spoken by an insane relative. No need to listen to that. Who are you now? Stay here. Stay right here and find out, who are you when all these things are put aside, including the wanting to be what you already are?

Well, I want to say these things intellectually.

Yes, so put that aside. That's also cuckoo banana.

What I suggest you do is bring your eyes here. Because then you can use this form as an anchor to what is real. You see, there's no "most of the time" here. There's no "work" and no "money." There's just your own Self looking back. This is very real, like a cold shower is real. Just keep your gaze here so you stay present in the room and find out who is looking now. Who is seeing Arjuna?

My Self.

My Self. Very good. What percentage of "my Self" are you? Fifty percent? Sixty percent?

One hundred percent.

One hundred percent my Self. Very nice. I am one hundred percent my Self. Look into "my Self" now and take a tape measure and see how big it is.

I don't believe I can measure it.

I don't believe I can measure it! Marvelous! I don't believe I can measure it. So it's infinite. "My Self" is infinite. How delicious. And tell me, this "my Self" which is infinite, was there a creation date?

No.

Is there any expiration date when it will run out?

I don't believe so.

Eternal. Infinite and eternal. Now, is this ninety-eight percent here, or one hundred percent here?

It's all here.

It's all here. Good. Now, what about this wanting to be my Self? Stay here. Stay right here and see if there is any wanting remaining for that which is one hundred percent here.

No.

No. Very good. Now tell me, can you rest as That which you are?

Can I rest?

Can you just be this? Let me give you a clue, okay? *(Whispers)* You have no choice about it. It's just a polite question.
Could you rest as This which you already are. Could you just be This?

I hope so.

Ohhh. *(Laughter)* Tell me something. Could you be in California right now?

Yes.

Any need for hope?

No.

No. If somebody says "I hope so," what kind of a person do we have?

A doubting person.

Well, the official word is cuckoo banana. *(laughter)* To hope to be where you already inevitably are is cuckoo banana, isn't it? So again, look back in your Self, —what's there?

Stay present. Don't go to thought. Just stay present and see, what is observing this?

That's hard to describe.

Beautiful. Any limits?

No.

Any beginning or ending in time?

No.

No. So here we are, back home on the ranch, okay? Now, try to make it go away. Try to get rid of This which is observing. You're allowed any trick you like.

Well, it's not going away, right now, anyway.

No. Right now, it can't go away.

My fear is that it will go away later on. My awareness of it will go away.

That's right, yes. Now what is "later on?"

Later on tonight or tomorrow.

But what is "later on tonight?" You see, this thing is called a tape recorder. Feel it. It's hard; it's real. This thing is called a watch. And this is a hand, feel the hand. These are called real things. Now tell me, what is "later on tonight?"

Well, I can't touch that.

No. Why not?

It's a different dimension.

Oh really? You've been watching too much Star Trek! *(Laughter)* So tell me, in which dimension is "later on tonight" real?

Some different point in time as I perceive it, I guess.

Well, where is this different point in time?

In the future.

Where's that?

It hasn't happened yet.

So where is it, now?

It doesn't exist right now.

(Claps hands) It doesn't exist. It does not exist. Not exist means not real. No more real than the monkeys sitting up on that top shelf brandishing guns. Anything to be afraid of? Are they any threat to your life?

No.

And what about this "later on tonight?" Anything to be afraid of?

No.

No. Any problem now?

No.

How About Now?

You see, the problem is this. It's very simple. The whole problem has to do with your uncle.

Say again?

I said the whole problem has to do with your uncle.

My uncle?

You have a crazy uncle in an insane asylum. You went there to visit your uncle and you could see he wasn't doing very well. He seemed to be feeling unhappy. You thought you could introduce him to reality, you see. So you asked the psychiatric nurse if you could take him out for the day to visit the mall and show him a good time. She said sure, but to take good care of him and to remember that he's crazy. That he's not capable of putting one coherent thought after another and he'll constantly tell you to do completely nutty things.

So here you are, wandering around the shopping mall with this guy just behind your shoulder, whispering all the time, *"Pickles, I like pickles. And yesterday there was smoked herring in my bed. Be careful! Monsters everywhere with guns. Something terrible is going to happen. And later on tonight there's going to be a problem. Or tomorrow. Better get to California as quick as you can! There's something wrong with the sky. Why is it so big? You better work really hard at trying to be what you already are, because you're not yourself yet."*

And he just carries on like that. But you are perfectly free not to listen to him. He's insane! You can have compassion. You can say to him, "It's okay. Sshhhh. Just relax. Everything is under control." And you are absolutely welcome not to listen to him. What else can you do? You've checked him out of the mental hospital and this is just how he is. Just don't listen to him.

Let me give you a clue about how to recognize when he's speaking to you. The clue is called thinking. Thinking itself is your crazy uncle. Anything that smacks of a belief or an idea, anything that smacks of a statement about the past or the future, anything that smacks of desire or fear is your uncle.

Is there anything left?

Yes! You know what's left? Delicious life is left! Delicious, entertaining, humorous, alive life is left. Good food is left. Beautiful, loving people are left. Glorious nature is left. Wonderful life is left for you to enjoy when you don't listen to your crazy uncle.

Thinking is always negative. If you don't pay attention to your uncle, there comes the recognition that you are already in paradise. You are already living in a world that is completely perfect, blessed, saturated in love.

There are times already, I'm sure, when you put your uncle aside and you feel at peace. At night when you go to sleep you put him aside for awhile and you sleep peacefully. At peak moments when you're really engaged in what's happening now, your uncle goes off for a walk. For example, when you're eating a really delicious meal, so delicious you stop thinking or talking, your uncle is gone and you enjoy yourself. When you're making love, hopefully you don't bring your uncle to bed with you! You leave him outside the room and enjoy yourself.

He's a bit tattered and threadbare and he has a penchant for failure. As far as he's concerned, he's married the wrong person, living in the wrong town, working at the wrong job, doesn't have enough money. He runs on a mantra. It's actually a sacred mantra in many traditions. A sacred, esoteric mantra. The basis of many religions. And the mantra is this: *"Everything is wrong as it is."*

Consequently, listening to your uncle, how can you possibly enjoy life? How can you experience love with your uncle present? How can you enjoy your job, or make money, or have a good relationship? Just tune him out. You don't have to listen. And then things are so simple.

You know, we're the same. We're both Westerners. We were both raised in similar cultures with similar difficulties. But there's a perk that comes from the work I'm in. I talk about this stuff so much that every now and then it rubs off on me. I got back from Boulder on Wednesday and I've just been here alone in the house for a few days. I can't describe how good I feel. It's nothing that we can't all have. I go up those stairs to the bed. I lie down. There's nothing going on, and yet it's ecstatic. It's unbelievably ecstatic for no reason at all. I haven't got a harem up there or anything. I don't have great financial fortunes. I don't have particularly great health, though it's not bad. I don't have any reason for feeling good. I don't even have anyone in the house with me. The less you listen to thought, the more it leaves you alone. The more you don't listen to your uncle, the more likely he's just going to find someone else to bug.

Does your uncle come to visit you from time to time?

Yes, and he's welcome. But I've learned that his ramblings are not a good basis for decision making of any kind. Twenty-four hours a day, just say no! Don't listen. Everyone has an insane relative. My good friend Catherine Ingram, one of the most honest teachers around today, she talks about an auntie in the same way. We all have mad relatives, but there is no obligation to listen to them.

Then you'll find that most of your interactions with people are just looking and loving. There's nothing to say, there's nothing to resolve, there's nothing to fix. There isn't a great need for words. You just look and sigh at the wonder of it all. And the funny thing is that truly, this is available now. It's just like flipping on a switch. It used to be that Indian gurus talked about this, with long beards and flowing robes. So here I am, this ordinary Westerner with kids and credit card debts and the whole Western frame of reference. How could I possibly aspire to the giddy heights of these teachers? But now, these days, it almost all Westerners speaking about this. There are almost no Indian teachers left. And it's Westerners with backgrounds just like yours. If it's possible for a tall, skinny Englishman from a dysfunctional background to stop listening to his uncle, it's possible for you, too.

What do I do when I find I'm listening to the crazy uncle?

Stop listening.

Okay. Just try to put my mind somewhere else?

No, he *is* your mind.

Oh, yeah. How do I stop listening?

How do you stop listening? By stopping listening. Stop giving it energy. Recognize that he's crazy, without any exceptions. We keep thinking that somehow each message might be something important. Not one in ten thousand thoughts is valuable information.

But there are things I need to do during the day. I need to plan them and organize my time. That's different from what you're talking about, isn't it?

Yes, there is a difference between impulse and thought. Impulse just arises. It's very clean. It's very peaceful. It just comes. The next thing to do becomes apparent. You don't have a list of things to do in a day; you've got one thing to do now or no things to do now.

What's wrong with a list?

If you're really troubled by this, write the list down and then it's done. But it's not about those kinds of thoughts. "I have to go to the post office" doesn't disturb your peace. It's "should I or shouldn't I," that disturbs peace — trying to figure it out, trying to plan. That's all based in desire and fear: desire for approval; desire for control; desire for love; fear of disapproval; fear of being out of control; fear of separation. It's all based in desire and fear. "I need to go to the post office" is not based in either desire or fear, it's a recognition that there are some letters on your desk that need stamps. Letters — stamps — post office — response. Things are so simple. I'm not saying anything that is of any great intelligence. It's so simple.

I want to be there with you.

You're already here with me. You're already perfectly at peace. You've just been listening to an insane uncle. You are not right now, and you're very happy about it.

How would you recognize the difference between impulse and addiction?

That's a really good question. It's for that reason that we have the work that we do. This is Satsang and for some people Satsang is enough. Addiction to anything, as far as I can see, mostly arises out of an incomplete willingness to feel. Some feeling state has arisen and there has been a flinching from it, an unwillingness to fully feel. And in the unwillingness to fully feel, it leaves this resistance in place, which causes tension. In that unwillingness to feel, there is this gnawing and that becomes addictive. It can be gnawing for love or gnawing for tobacco or gnawing for whatever, you see. The antidote for that is simply to restore the full capacity to feel, which is what we do in the weekend Satsang Intensives. We spend a weekend basically restoring one's capacity to fully feel experience, so much so that it evaporates. When you fully feel anything it disappears. It's half-digested experience that causes addiction. Addiction will evaporate when the ability to feel is restored and there is no aspect of experience that is being flinched from.

Unfortunately, not everyone realizes that this means business, what we're talking here. Satsang is not a hobby. It's a way of living life. Unless it is adopted as a way of living life, I would recommend going to the movies instead of Satsang. I don't see any point in Satsang unless you're going to go for it hook, line and sinker. Do you know what I mean? Here's my recommendation. When I met Papaji, I felt like, "What the hell, nothing else has worked, let's try this." And I gave it everything. I wrote him a letter and I said to him, "I'm perfectly happy to die, physically, if that is what is required to rest as This. I have no attachment to anything, including the body." And I meant it. I was perfectly willing to die. And it worked. But it has to be one hundred percent. There is no idea of preparation or gradual transition involved in this. You just recognize, once and for all, that the mind is insane. *Insane*. All desire is insane. It's all seeking for that which you already have, you see. Seeking for love outside, when you *are* love. It's a rare thing for people to understand what this really means. It doesn't mean seventy percent of the mind's activity is insane and the other thirty percent is worth following. It means all desire and fear is insane. All thoughts of "I want this and I don't want that" are insane. It doesn't mean there's no activity. Activity can arise but the activity is no longer dictated by your insane uncle. It's dictated by a response to what is present.

So tell me, is there any wanting left now? Anything left to attain? Anything left incomplete?

No.

Sure?

Right now there isn't, but I don't know about another moment.

Go to another moment than this one. Try to get out of right now. I'll stay here in right now and watch. You go to another moment; I want to see how you do it.

Did you do it yet?

I'm staying with you now.

Do you have any choice?

No.

You see, right now is all you've got. Try to go somewhere else — you can't. Try to be somewhere other than here, you can't. There's no choice. You've got a menu and there's one item on it. Here and Now soup. That's it! That's all they serve.

(Laughter) So just relax. The choice has already been made. You are nailed to the here and now. Nailed. *(Laughter)* You can't get out of it. Try!

How About Now?

I don't want to get out of it.

You can't.

Good.

The choice is not whether to be here, now, in this moment. There's no choice about that. The choice is whether you're going to spend this moment enjoying what is real or listening to an insane relative. And you've probably gathered by now what my recommendation is.

I'd rather be real, because my uncle is very insane.

Everyone's uncle is insane. There's really only one uncle. It's called the collective mind. It's a funny thing when you start to look around. The human condition is really a bizarre story. Everyone is running around in circles trying to acquire things or experiences that never bring them the happiness they thought it would. It's absolute masochism, you see. Everyone is running around trying to get external love, and what a mess that brings. You get it, and then you're running around in circles trying to get away from it again. *(Laughter)* Meanwhile, you can rest and be love itself. And your own Self in form will come to you for refuge. Everyone is running around in circles trying to get wealth. And then they get it and have to spend it all in treating their ulcers, which they acquired in the amassing of the wealth. Or, you can rest in gratitude for what is, and richness will come to you in every moment. Everyone's running around in circles trying to get wisdom and enlightenment. Are you ready to die to all that?
Yes.

Is it done?

Yes, this works great.

It's not because the work that I do works, it's because *you* work. When you relax into who you really are, you work great. So it's a very rewarding thing just to restore people back to their natural state. And they go, "Wow, this is great!" What we do on the weekends is just restore your capacity to have natural experience. And your natural state is free. Your natural state is flowing—which also means your natural state is no problem. Your natural state is creative response coming naturally to life. Your natural response is love. You are naturally loving. You don't have to be taught to love.

You are naturally loving and giving and good,
And perfect and supremely Divine.
You are all That.
You are naturally the source of all wisdom.
You don't need a guru.
It's not necessary.
You are already everything.
Just remove a little flinching
From the things that cause resistance
And you can just fall back into your Self.
Then things are simple—
Unless you listen to your uncle again.
Then it gets complicated.
But you can always stop listening to your uncle
And things become simple again.

12

Start at the End

If you try to dissolve all resistance first,
It becomes very complicated.
Start with the conclusion of the journey.
Begin where spiritual work ends.

Start with being awake.

Then once you have a good sense of things—
The tables are turned up the right way,
The teakettle is no longer balancing on its nose,
The glasses are put back in their right places—
Then you can see what's what.
You can clean a little better.

Start with waking;
Then clean house.

13

The Clue

It is as though
God has left a huge clue
Right across the top of everything;
Like a crossword puzzle
With the answer blazed in neon.

Sky is the immense clue
As to the nature of things —
Vast, empty, spacious, ever present, subtle.

Look as far as you like to find the limit.

Notice the quiet yet triumphant banner
Of your heart's song blasted in neon across the sky.

14

The Mutuality of Wakefulness

I am not a guru.
I have no interest in gurus.
I am not interested at all.
I am passionately interested in
Mutuality in wakefulness—
That we can sit together as friends,
You and I,
And lay all our cards on the table.
I'm sure you have your difficulties in life,
You have your emotions.
People have difficulties with money,
Relationships and health.
I've got the same stuff, too.
And all of that is floating
In the great Mystery.

We share it all.

I know many of the contemporary teachers,
Having become a kind of teacher myself,
Having been asked by Papaji
To represent the Truth.
I would never be doing this
If he hadn't insisted;
But he did.
So now I get to know other people who teach,
Both on his behalf, and others.
And everyone is the same, I tell you.
It may look different

Because when someone's sitting giving Satsang
They don't always talk a lot
About their own life;
They talk the absolute Truth.
But I tell you,
Scratch below the surface,
Get to know people behind the scenes
And everyone is the same.
In relationships
Everyone goes through the same stuff.
When there's not enough money
Everyone lives through the same concerns.
When the body gets sick
Everyone has the same kind of experience.
It's called being a human being.
There's nothing wrong with it.
Common to all this sea of humanity
There is something underneath—
Waiting—
It is who you are already,
Who we all already are.
And that doesn't require achieving anything
Or changing your relationship to anything at all.

Papaji has been my sweetheart.
He is the one who blew the whistle
On the whole game.
But then he had the grace
And the compassion
To let me see him as a human being.
I lived for a period in his house;
I had breakfast with him in the morning,
I went to see him in Satsang,
Then we'd go back and have lunch.
I realized this guy had every emotion
That I didn't accept in myself.

How About Now?

Every thought,
Every kind of prejudice
That I thought was so terrible
In myself,
He demonstrated to me.
But what I noticed about him was
The tendency to make it wrong
Never arose in him.
If anger came in him,
Whoosh!
It would come,
Pass through,
And disappear without a trace.

This ended up being the greatest teaching.

I have had so many teachers,
So many great enlightened ones,
Sitting on a podium,
With cameras pointing,
Doing that whole guru number.
And what did that create?
Separation.

Then I met him.
Many people wanted to create
A mega-guru situation for him, too.
He refused until the last short period.
Fifty years he refused.
He was simple, ordinary.
There was such compassion in that
Because it bursts all your expectations.
In his profound ordinariness,
In his getting upset with things,
I realized that his being awake
Has nothing to do

With which kind of emotions arise
Or which kind of thoughts come.
It only has to do with
Leaving it all alone,
Letting it be in its natural simplicity.
Many people were shocked
By how ordinary he let himself be,
And they ran away in righteous indignation.
But if you could really relax into just seeing it,
It would be more liberating
Than any other teaching could be;
Because finally his ordinariness —
His ordinary humanity —
Was the greatest teaching.

Leave yourself alone.
When you can let your teacher
Be ordinary and have bad moods,
You can let yourself be ordinary
And have bad moods too.

This letting yourself be
Allows you to relax into
Simple sanity,
Into the peace the Heart has always longed for.

15

Relax Preference

A knife cutting through a melon cannot leave one half.

Can you see that attachment to Grace
Or an enlightenment experience
Must bring in its wake mental activity?

A preference has been established.

When a melon is cut into two pieces,
Two halves remain.
If you slice reality into enlightenment,
Which is opposed to thoughts,
Duality and a wave of mental activity arise in its wake.

Just now,
Relax the preference for Grace over thoughts;
Welcome mental reactivity and Grace equally.
Perhaps you could stretch your arms wide enough
So that both the good child and the bad child
Are equally loved.

Then what is being spoken of is just the song of your own heart.
Everything is equally embraced.

16

Give Up the Struggle

You are already That for which you are seeking.
All that is required to know this
Is to give up the struggle.
It is so simple.
And when I say give up the struggle,
It doesn't mean you don't get stressed anymore.
This is so simple,
So undeniable.
Emotions coming and going are not a problem.
Strong emotions come
And disappear again.
Strong thoughts come
And disappear again.
There is only one tiny thing
That could possibly create a problem
In any of that,
And it's such a tiny thing,
You can pop it with a tiny pin.
The only thing that could interfere
With everything being natural and relaxed
Is the idea that
You shouldn't have this stuff going on.
That tiny idea,
"I shouldn't have this emotion,
I shouldn't have this thought,"
Creates this wall within yourself
And then the sense of presence is lost.
The thoughts coming and the emotions coming
Are not a problem.
What is a thought?

HOW ABOUT NOW?

It is an imaginary object.
It is something that does not exist.
It has no power.
Something that is imaginary
Has no power over you.
The only power it could possibly have
Is that you go into resistance to it.
If you fantasize that the object is real
You could suffer.
But the imaginary object itself
Will never hurt you.
How can something you have already recognized
To be an illusionary object affect you,
Except if you resist it?
A thought cannot hurt you.
A thought cannot touch you.
It has no power over you.
Beyond this
What is left
That is real
To hurt you
In this moment?

17

Marriage

Sing the song of this moment,
Instead of the chorus of "What Might Happen,"
The litanies of "Sometimes" and "On Occasion" and "I
Remember."

Sing the song of the perfection of Now.
Offer your hand.
Deepen your marriage to This Moment.

18

Who Wants to be Enlightened

When I met my teacher
I was very preoccupied
With spiritual seeking.
I wanted to become "enlightened."
Now I'm not sure what that word means,
But that's what I wanted then.
It was actually a way of saying
I wanted to escape from
The suffering, constant change and turmoil
Of being a human being.
I went to see him and told him
I wanted to be free of seeking.

Instead of saying,
"Okay here's how to do it;
Recite this mantra
Or do these yoga postures,"
He simply asked everyone
The same question:
"Who is it that wants to be free?
Who is the one seeking
For some spiritual state?"

This question is usually overlooked.
Who is this one?
Who is this person
Involved in spiritual practice,
Trying to achieve something
That is not yet achieved?

Later my father came to India.
He is a British journalist
Properly educated at Oxford.
He met my teacher and liked him.
After a few days he had to ask me
The inevitable question:
"Why are you not just getting on
With a normal life?
Why are you here in India
With all this dirt and chaos,
Living with a guru?
Why aren't you doing something useful?"
I said to him,
"We are usually so busy in life,
Doing this and that,
We never stop long enough to ask,
'Who am I?'
Who is the one here?'"
I said to him,
"Daddy, who are you?"
And he gave a response
That sums it up for all of us.
He said,
"One simply doesn't ask oneself
That kind of question!
Why would you want to know that?
Why is that so important?"

Recognizing why this is so important,
May be the most important question now
For this entire species on this planet.
This may sound a little fanatic,
But I'm of the opinion
That the very survival of life
On this planet

How About Now?

Rests in the simple question,
"Who Am I?"

We have been chasing after more money,
More happiness,
More sex with more people,
More this,
More that,
Without asking who is it
That is chasing after all these things.
"Who am I?"

If you go to an art gallery
And see a beautiful painting,
Say, the "Mona Lisa"
Or a Botticelli angel,
You might look at that painting
And find it very beautiful
And feel deeply touched.
But someone else might walk
Into the art gallery,
Look at the same painting
And not like it at all.
So where is the beauty?
Our normal day-to-day experience
Tells us that the beauty
Is in the painting,
But that cannot be,
Or everyone would see the same beauty
In the same paintings.
Where is the beauty,
Where is the origin of beauty?

It must be in That
Which perceives the painting.
Otherwise everyone would find

The same thing beautiful.
It is within you, projected out.

The same is true when you love someone
Very deeply.
What is the source,
What is the cause of the love?
We want to say the love is caused
By the presence of the other.
But not everyone will find your beloved
As beautiful as you do,
Or feel the same love and intimacy.
At least you'd better hope not!
The love is coming from within you.
It is projected out.

In the investigation of this question,
"Who am I?"
In the total absorption
Of attention back into your Self,
The source of love,
The source of happiness,
The source of peace is revealed.
This is not only the end
Of seeking and unnecessary struggle for you,
Or for me,
But for the world we live in —
For our children.
This world is characterized by separation,
By me against you.
I win; I get more money so you get less —
Competition.
As long as we overlook
The real source of happiness and peace,
There never seems to be enough.
We always feel lack,

HOW ABOUT NOW?

Striving for more.
We are willing to sacrifice forests
To get more money.

Satsang means to turn our attention
Back to the real source of happiness.
We break the addiction
To looking outside.
We no longer have to create
Enormous physical houses
To create security.
You can feel secure in the awareness
of who you truly are.
This is the purpose of Satsang.

19

Already Here

It's really very simple,
Everyone's birthright;
It can't be denied once it's seen.
A very simple, ordinary, relaxing, cozy thing —
Your own true nature, your own true heart,
Already here.

To overlook this thing, this no-thing,
Is to unnecessarily suffer,
Is to unnecessarily become identified and trapped
By what was originally intended to be a fun game —
The diversity of form.

To recognize this no-thing again,
To awaken to your true nature,
Is to slip comfortably out of the trap of identity
And to find that the source of all happiness,
The source of all love,
The source of all beauty,
Is You.

20

No Preparation Required

*Y*ou say that you were searching for twenty years before you met your teacher and gave up the search. How do you know that all the twenty years didn't play a role in your reaching that moment where you just decided to be in the moment? How do you know that maybe that wasn't necessary to get to that place where you jumped off the cliff?

Suppose your glasses are sitting on your nose, but you have the idea," I've lost my glasses." You look under the sofa—not there. You look under the cushions—not there. You look under your bed, you look on top of the medicine cabinet, you look in all the kitchen cabinets, you look in your car, you look in the garden; you conduct a thorough search everywhere for three hours. Finally you sit down in exhaustion and discover that they were on your nose all that time. You realize that you were looking *through* that for which you were seeking. Then somebody says to you, "How do you know that the three hours of searching in all the wrong places wasn't, in fact, necessary for you to find them on your nose?"

It's a good question, because it was only after those three hours of searching that you were exhausted enough to sit down on the sofa and discover them on your nose. It is a good question; one doesn't know. I can just tell you that there is actually no preparation necessary. By coincidence, it may be that the common sequence of events is that people look everywhere in order to give up looking everywhere and discover that what they were looking for they had all along. But actually, the truth is, it's not necessary. It's not necessary to look through the whole house to find that they were on your nose. You could have found that at the beginning.

Buddha was faced once with the same question. He was born as a prince, Siddhartha. When he was born, the Vedic astrologer who came, said to his father, "This prince will either be a great spiritual renunciate, or he will become a great ruler." The king, his father, replied, "We'd better make sure that he's a ruler." So the astrologer said, "Well, make sure that he never sees death or decay, because once he sees the ephemeral nature of this world, he won't have any attachment left." The story goes on to say that he grew up and married a beautiful bride, Yashodara, the most beautiful woman in the land. They had a son and named him Rahula. Siddhartha had everything going for him. He was the prince of the kingdom. He had fancy cars, color TV, cellular phones, everything. Then one day, to cut a very long story short, he went out with his charioteer, Ananda. "Take me outside the palace gates," he said. Inside the palace everyone was young; nobody was allowed in there over forty-five because they didn't even want him to see gray hairs. But he said to Ananda, "Take me out." Ananda said, "I don't think I should, my lord. We've been instructed not to." "Ananda, I am your lord. Take me out," insisted Siddhartha. So they went out and the first thing they saw was someone who was sick. Siddhartha asked, "What's the matter with that guy?" Ananda replied, "He is sick, my lord." "Sick!" exclaimed the prince. "Will I ever get sick?" Ananda replied, "Yes, it is possible you will get sick, my lord." Siddhartha sat back in his chariot. He had never considered this aspect of life.

They continued their travels outside the palace walls and came upon a very old man—stooped and withered. "What's happened to him?" the prince asked. The charioteer replied, "He's old, my lord, a very old man." "Will I get old?" asked Siddhartha. "You will surely get old, my lord," replied Ananda.

The next thing they saw was a funeral procession. Coffins are not used in India; the dead body is just carried on a stretcher with flowers. "Well, what happened to that guy?" asked the prince once more. "He's dead, my lord," came the reply. "Will I also die?" inquired the prince. "Yes, surely you will die, my lord."

Finally, they saw a renunciate sitting under a tree wearing orange and looking very glowing. Siddhartha asked, "What's up with that guy?" And Ananda replied, "He has renounced the world." Siddhartha fell silent.

That night the prince went home. He stood at the threshold of his bedroom door and saw his beautiful wife, Yashodara, lying there asleep with their baby. This is a very poignant moment—a moment that everyone comes to—a moment that I myself have come to. He stood there on the threshold, pulled one way toward his family life and his responsibilities, and the other way toward his longing for freedom.

He chose to leave his old life behind (which actually, these days, is not really necessary), but he chose to leave the whole thing. He began trying everything in his search for freedom. He cut his hair. He exchanged his beautiful prince's robes for beggar's clothing. For six years he did everything he could find: Primal Therapy, EST, Rolfing, Scientology, everything that was available, he tried. He hung upside down from a tree. He stared at the moon for three days. Everything he could find, he tried it.

Finally, he got to the point that everyone will get to sooner or later. That's the invitation here tonight—to bring yourself to this point. He had been fasting; that was his latest thing. He was just eating a few grains of hemp seed a day and by now he was really skinny. He had fallen into the river and hardly had the strength to pull himself out. Finally, a woman showed up. She said to him, "What on earth is the matter with you? You look terrible!" And he said, "Oh, I'm a holy man. I'm fasting." And she said, "Don't be ridiculous. Have some yogurt." (The moral of this story is: listen to women. They've got their heads screwed on much better than us guys.) She said, "Give it up, have some yogurt." It woke him up from the trance of masochism called spiritual seeking. So he wandered over to a tree, a *bodhi* tree, and sat down. I'm going to quote the original Pali scripture here, a translation thereof. He sat down under the tree and he said, "Screw this." That's what he said. He sat down and he said, "Screw this; I've had it." That's the point you have to get to. "I'm done, man; I'm cooked. That's it."

He sat down, closed his eyes and said, "I'm not getting up from this tree until it's done, whatever it is — I don't even know anymore — but whatever it is, I'm not getting up from this tree until it's over."

He only had to stay there one night.

I tell you, it doesn't even take a night. Right here in this room at 8:42 p.m. — if you make up your mind that by 8:43 p.m. seeking's done, seeking is done. Siddhartha sat down and during the night, he came to recognize that what he had been seeking for was who he actually already was. That is all. Mara, the incarnation of desire and multi-level marketing, came to tempt him and said, "Come, come, come." He looked Mara right in the eyes and said, "I know you are a creation of my own mind. I know that you are no more real than my thoughts." And Mara disappeared. The illusion was cracked, you see, as soon as he realized that it was all created out of mind. Then he recognized that he was already what he had been seeking and always had been. He had always been Buddha, which means Consciousness.

Here's the point of the story that I'm coming to. He went back to Sarnath to his buddies. They took one look at him and said, "Jesus, Sid, what happened to you?" because he looked so different; he looked so shiny. His answer is very significant. He said, "Nothing happened to me under the *bodhi* tree — nothing. That's why it can be called supreme, absolute enlightenment — because nothing happened. I stopped waiting for something to happen."

Years later he went back to the Sakyamuni Kingdom where he had been the prince and Yashodara, his wife, was there. By now she had gray hair and their son was a teenager. She came out of the palace with a rolling pin in her hand. "Where have you been all these years? You are my husband." He said, "Well, I have reached the end of the search." And she said, "Couldn't you have attained what you have attained here with me and Rahula in the castle?" He replied, "Yes, actually I could have. I probably wouldn't have, but I could have."

This is the answer to your question. It is not *necessary* to spend years seeking in order to recognize that you have always been this. The actual sequence of events seems to be that one *does* go through seeking and exhausts the seeking, and then one realizes in retrospect that one didn't need the seeking after all. Somehow you have to try it to realize you don't need it. Who's to say if it's necessary or not?

Something is happening now. I can't even tell you how I know this, but I know it. I know it like one knows anything without any doubt. I travel all over the country. I go to two or three cities a month, like this. I also travel in Europe and it's the same everywhere I go. All over the world, realization is happening — the same realization that we read about in the *Upanishads*, in the *Bhagavad Gita*, in the *Vedas*. The same level of realization is happening now to ordinary people. I don't know why. Perhaps we have all our teachers to thank for preparing the ground. Something incredible is occurring now. I can't justify this to you; it is something beyond justification. Anyone who wants to recognize freedom now can have it now — anyone — regardless of their preparation. I have met people and worked with people who have no preparation at all. A carpenter who had never even read a spiritual book, came to see me because he heard me on the radio and somehow was touched. I looked into his eyes and I said, "Never mind about all this stuff. Who are you in this moment?" He recognized who he really is, he woke up, and it didn't go away. And he had never meditated once.

The habit of seeking can become an impediment after awhile, instead of a help, because one gets professional at it. One gets so good at doing practices and so caught up in the nitty gritty of it that one forgets why the practices were even started in the first place.

The frequency of Consciousness is changing very rapidly and dramatically everywhere, and the whole planet is moving into that intensity. You don't see it, but when I went to see Poonjaji in 1991, almost no one around him had had this recognition in any sort of stable way. Very few. With me, it took six days of him hammering, and I was already on fire. He told me later that he was working on me all night that final night. And I was, I would say, fairly ripe. Now it's 1998, only seven years later, and exactly the same thing that occurred for me in 1991 can happen for people now in an hour. So something is rapidly, rapidly, rapidly accelerating. You can't measure it, but as I travel from place to place I see that there is a rapid and dramatic lifting of the veil. I have other friends who are also teaching in this way and they see the same thing occurring. I would estimate that within a few years there will be millions of people fully realized on this planet. By fully realized, I just mean having given up seeking. That's all that realized really means. You give up seeking and *realize* that you've always been what you've been seeking for. It doesn't mean attaining anything. That's why it's called self-realization, not self-attainment. You realize what a dummy you've been—that you've been That all along. That's what realization is. You realize that you've been barking up the wrong tree.

It's happening and it's happening now—maybe because things have never been so unstable physically, economically, environmentally. Maybe our days are numbered; I don't know. Once you realize freedom, it doesn't matter. Once you recognize that you're not the body—that you're Consciousness—the whole thing could go up in smoke tomorrow and nothing's lost. This is just stuff; it's nothing. The love remains intact whether there's manifestation or not. So maybe it's the instability of the environment now that's causing this acceleration. Maybe there are packs of angels flying around showering dust, I don't know. But what I can tell you is, now's the time.

Take it from me. There are no possible grounds for postponement. If you haven't earned the right by now, you never will.

21

Wipe the Altar Clean

Take the altar of your life and wipe everything off of it:
Great relationships, security, nice house, money, the right job.

Leave the marble of your altar so clean,
Not even one speck of dust is there.

Dedicate your altar to emptiness of Heart,
Fullness of Love.

Finally,
When the altar is swept clean,
These things come back as fringe benefits.

Not if you want them,
Not if you strike a deal.

It won't work.

Leave the altar completely free.
Give yourself over to Divine Will,

And then see what happens.

22

A Natural Response to Life

In Satsang I feel completely at peace. Then when I go home I get caught up in looking after my kids, and I lose peace.

If you truly surrender
To the flow of life,
You surrender not only
To external events,
You surrender also to whatever arises
Within you
To meet those events.
If there are children there, so be it.
To resist the fact that
The children need to be taken care of
Would be a "doing."
To resist a book getting written
If it's bursting forth
Would be a "doing."
To resist an attraction to something
Would be a "doing."

There is truly no inside or outside.
It is all just Consciousness playing.
Let it play.
Then there is a naturalness —
There is a biological naturalness that occurs.
This is a human monkey
And it has a natural instinct
To take care of its offspring.
Why resist that?

HOW ABOUT NOW?

How is the desire to take care of one's children different from spiritual seeking? Isn't that just more seeking?

There is a totally different kind of desire.
On one hand
There is the desire to have more money
So that we can have more stuff and more security.
It is basically a distortion of
The longing to come home.
"I want peace.
I want to relax.
I want to know who I am.
And I want to get more money so that
I can relax and be at peace later."
A natural desire to come home
Gets projected onto external events.

On the other hand
There is just the natural responding to life.
The oil in the car gets changed
Because the oil in the car needs changing.
It's just the flow of life —
Black sticky life, but life.
You don't need to resist
A natural response to life.
The idea "I shouldn't have desire"
Is just another imposition.
There is a difference between
The natural responding to life
From natural Presence
And the trying to get Presence
From various experiences.
Wanting to make tons of money
Because you feel lack
Is a totally different thing.

I find that my work as a publisher is often very distracting for me.

Once you rest in who you are,
Once you know who you are,
Life still goes on.

It doesn't mean that
You sit in a cave
And nothing ever happens any more.
This is actually
The amazing,
Fascinating,
Exciting challenge
We have as Western human beings now.
The model for wakefulness in India
And other oriental countries
Has been a model of renunciation.
Read a book like Stephen Mitchell's
Enlightened Heart, or *Enlightened Mind*.
Almost everyone in these books
Is a monk or a recluse.
Now it's changing.
Now it's ordinary people
Like you and me,
With children and jobs,
Who are waking up
In the midst of ordinary life.
The true and honest investigation
Into all this
Will liberate you from every imposition,
Will leave you free, without any models,
Without trying to be
Indian or Hindu or Tibetan or whatever,
And just leave you as natural Jimmie.

How About Now?

Jimmie becomes
The contemporary Buddha.
Now, instead of having to
Look to Buddha , 2,500 years ago,
For a way to do all this,
We look to Jimmie.
Jimmie, the publisher,
Jimmie, the Buddha,
Driving his Nissan to his publishing house.
This is the contemporary model of awakening.
This whole thing needs to be given a fresh context
Because six billion people on the planet
Are not going to become monks.
It is not necessary to abandon anything
Pertaining to a normal life.
The challenges
And the difficulties
Of ordinary life
Make this Presence
Stronger and stronger.

Look around right now
And share this Presence.
Let yourself be That now.

23

Embrace Everything

If you try to divide life
Into what is spiritual and what is not,
Dual and non-dual,
This creates a kind of cripple —
A cripple who is trying
To avoid the ordinariness of life.

If you embrace it all,
It takes more courage,

But it is a fuller life you are left with.
Embrace everything.

24

Freedom from the Need
to be Free

There is a freedom
Even from the need to be free,
Even from the need to try to be spiritual.
This is beyond
The duality of awake and asleep,
Enlightened and unenlightened.
This is relaxation into the suchness of things
Just the way they are.

You have a bad moment —
What's wrong with that?
You have a negative thought —
Who cares?
It is all occurring in something that does not change.
Just experiment,
For the benefit of the doubt,
By simply leaving yourself alone.
Try not picking the scab anymore.
Just let yourself be
And see what happens.
This is beyond the need to try to be awake —
Beyond ambition.

So much of what we take to be spiritual
Is just another kind of ambition.
We want money,
Or more sex

Or a bigger house,
Or a better career,
And finally, we think we've gone beyond all that
Because now we want enlightenment.
It's just another ambition.
It's no different from wanting any of the rest of it.
It's just another egotistical dream.
If you let go of that, things are as they are.
And who's to say
You shouldn't have moods,
Or thoughts?
Who's to say you should be this way or that?

It is only the resistance that creates the suffering.
Even grief,
Incredible grief,
Has a sweetness
If you don't resist it;
It takes you deep into your Self.
Losing a lot of money,
The disappointment of that,
Can take you deep into your Self.
Just in relaxing into what is,
There is another doorway into the blessedness.
Only the resistance disturbs peace,
All resistance arises from concepts.
Resistance is a function of,
"It should be like this;
It should be like that…"
Ideas of what "spiritual" means.

Surrender all concepts
And you sit in the lap of the Gods.

25

What is in the Way of Finding?

When I first met Papaji, in the very first conversation I had with him, I asked him a question. At that time he was relatively unknown—there were probably half as many people there as are here tonight. There was just a little group. He was sitting on a bench with a mat on it in a sparsely furnished room, his living room. He was looking a bit bored, staring off into the distance. There were maybe eight or ten Western people sitting on the floor, very quiet. He had very long tea breaks at that time, about an hour. As a new arrival, I was called into his bedroom to see him. I was a very serious boy, a serious seeker. So I went to see him and I said, "I feel like I have been seeking as long as I can remember, most of this life, seeking, seeking, seeking." And I asked him, "What is in the way of giving up this search and finding?" He looked at me and lifted his eyebrows, like it was the most ridiculous question he had ever been asked in his whole life. "What is in the way of finding? Why, seeking, of course."

It was like he had taken up the rug and pulled. My entire universe collapsed because I realized the whole effort, all the questions, all the striving to become something else, all the practice, all the grasping to have a different experience than that which we already have—everything was all counterproductive. It was all ambition. And it was all overshadowing the inevitable truth of what is right here. Even right now, in this moment, That which is being sought is already absolutely present. Whether you label yourself enlightened or unenlightened, awake or unawake, or whatever; That which is being sought is already here. All that is necessary is to truly give up the ambition of trying to achieve something else. Then it is revealed. So simple, so simple. Whether you are in perfect balance or are absolutely neurotic, it doesn't matter.

26

The Individual is Doomed

The person you have taken yourself to be
Is doomed.
There is no way in eternity
That the person you think you are
Could ever be enlightened.

Why?
Because there's no one there!
Then what is left?
Only Consciousness;

Which has always been enlightened,
Which has always been full of love,
Which has always been perfect.

There has only ever been
One state of Consciousness,
And that is Consciousness itself.

You are That.

27

The Wave is Already Wet

The veil that hides this Secret
Is becoming so thin
It can be easily torn now by anyone.
It all comes down to what you value.

Value emptiness above content
And you are free.
Value peace above drama
And you are at rest.
Value not knowing above concepts
And you are wisdom itself.
Value love above relationships
And you are bathed in love.
So simple.

If you hold the idea,
"I can't get this,"
You create an unnecessary barrier.

It would be like a wave in the ocean saying,
"Oh, I don't know,
I see all the other waves
But I just don't think I can be wet.
There are some really big waves out here
But could I,
Little me,
With all my frothy foam,
Could I really be the Ocean?"

Dive deeply.
Become immersed in your Self!

28

The Mind is a Trickster

You know the story of Jesus
And the forty days and forty nights
And the devil?
What did the devil offer?
"I'm going to make you powerful."
But Jesus had the courage
And the wisdom
To say "No thanks,
I'm going to stay home with God."
That means, "I'm going to rest in Presence."
The same thing happened to Buddha.

All the cool dudes,
They say the same thing
When the devil mind comes around.

When Buddha sat under the *bodhi* tree,
Mara appeared,
Another version of the same devil.
Mara said the same thing,
"I will give you everything."
And Buddha, the dude, said,
"I know that you are a creation of my own mind."
Mara disappeared
And there was silence.

Just be a little aware.
This mind is a trickster.
What it's offering you
Always looks so good.
"C'mon, I'll give you this,

How About Now?

I'll give you that."
But it's all multi-level marketing.
Watch out.
Haven't you been taken on enough rides?
It is never like it's advertised in the brochures.

Read the small print very carefully
Before signing up for a ride.
You have everything you need at home.
You have such a great home,
The sweetest beloved
Anyone could ever find
Lives right in your house.
All the entertainment,
Everything is here,
Right at home.

Let the devil mind yack away.
No one says you have to listen.

29

Invisible Secret

As long as things are perceived
Through the filters of thought and concept,
What all this is pointing to
Simply doesn't exist.

You can see the fruits,
The consequences,
But you can't see It.

It may bring more peace
But it is beyond peace.
It may bring more laughter
But it is beyond laughter.

You can just abandon interest in all else
And THIS is what is left.

You don't have to give up anything—
The nitty gritty of ordinary life can continue.
It *must* continue.

But when life is lived
From this invisible secret
Everything else falls magically into place around it.

30

Energy and Conciousness

Question: What is the relationship of the subtle body or the energetics of the universe to this sense of "I" and the existence of vibrations? How does that affect consciousness?

It doesn't;
Nothing affects Consciousness.
Some things we notice or not,
As we choose,
And some things we imagine or not,
As we choose.
Of course there is energy,
But don't get that mixed up
With freedom,
With wakefulness,
With the awakening to your true nature.
It has no connection,
Nothing to do with it.
You can become very interested in kundalini
And all that stuff—
There is no connection.
Wakefulness is the recognition of That
Which is here; which is now.

Whether you have been studying chi,
Or chi kung,
Or cheese;
It is all the same.
Not to say there is anything wrong with it.
If you want to understand the way

Energy moves in the body
And if you want to produce longevity,
It's perfectly okay,
Like changing the oil in the car.
But don't think it has
Something to do with freedom
Because you will be misled.
Some of it is nice for healing the body,
But if what you want is wakefulness
It is best not to get too distracted,
Because you can confuse the two.

As you probably know,
The human imagination can create
All kinds of weird things.
You can have fun with the mind,
But be careful!

This busy mind can take you
On some really wicked adventures.
It always looks so good.
Whether it's interest in etheric bodies,
Or whether it's making loads of money,
Or whether it's a new relationship,
These ships always sink.
All ships eventually sink.

Rest as the Ocean itself
And you will never sink again.

31

Rest Here

Relax back into who you really are.
You are Magnificence itself.

Let go of resistance to everything,
And what remains is the perfect flow
Of effortless Life.

What you are unwilling to feel
Remains as tension,
Becomes a gnawing,
Grows into addiction.

Restore the capacity to feel fully,
To allow all experience without flinching,
And the addiction,
The gnawing,
The tension,
Dissolve.

Rest here and things are simple.

32

Drop in First

When mind is faced with limitlessness,
It thinks, "Get out quick. Leave.
Don't stay here!"

When Heart is faced with limitlessness,
It says, "Ah, a hot tub!"
It perceives eternal life.

The trick with resistance, you see,
Is to drop first into the Heart.

33

Listen to the Heart

It depends on what you listen to.
If you listen to thoughts,
There is resistance.

If you listen to the Heart,
You fall into Home,
Like a dewdrop slipping from a leaf.

34

It's Different Now

It's almost impossible to find the right words to speak about what's happening now on this planet. For millennia this phenomenon of awakening, freedom, Self-realization, has been the realm of recluses and monks—people leading lives very different from our own. Just take a look in the metaphysical section of your local bookstore; everyone we have as a reference for enlightenment or awakening has led a very unusual life. Though there have been a few exceptions, like Kabir, this has been the context in which wakefulness has mostly occurred.

It is almost impossible to grasp what is occurring. It's different now. When I first met Papaji in 1991 it would take a long time for people to wake up. They would come and see him and it would be necessary for some kind of a hammering to occur for them to shift into wakefulness. But things are moving so quickly now that what happened as recently as 1991 is no longer a context for what is happening now in 1998. We don't realize this because it creeps up on us. It's like having a child; the child is born and grows imperceptibly day by day as the months and years pass. Then the relatives come after two or three years and say, "Oh my God, who's this?" It's nothing like the baby they saw two or three years ago, but because you're living with the child every day you don't realize the growth that has occurred. It's the same with the collective consciousness; we don't realize what's occurring. We try to use old models, old concepts, old parameters to understand what's happening now, and it doesn't fit.

It's important to understand this, because everything is different now. The atmosphere has become so much thinner. It's as though we're suddenly living at a higher altitude, whereas a few years ago it was more dense. I know this from conducting these meetings over the years, first seeing what people would go through to come to awakening and how unstable that awakening often was. A fireworks display would often come with the awakening because it was so contradictory to the dominant consciousness. Now, in 1998, it's all changed. People just slip into the same realization, the same wakefulness, the same blessedness, the same unconditional love that Buddha lived. And then if we try to use any of the old models to understand this, we doubt what's occurring. We doubt the validity of what's happening because it seems too easy. We say, "Wait a minute! Where are the fireworks? Where's this great traumatic experience I read about with Swami Atmanandaji? Where's the great dramatic torturing of the body that I read about in Krishnamurti's biography? Where's the fanfare of angels that I read about somewhere?" No, today it can be—swish—just like that! Because the shift is so small. The dominant consciousness has opened such a wide doorway that the whole planet is slipping into something. You can find it everywhere now.

I was in Austin, Texas, recently. In the evening there was a gathering, but no one knew me there. Here were ordinary people, housewives, carpenters. Maybe they'd done the Course in Miracles, or a 12-Step program or something, but there wasn't an established Satsang following there. Even so, many people already knew what I was talking about because they'd experienced it in their ordinary lives. They might have been hiking and something timeless and expansive had happened to them; maybe they had taken the dog for a walk and the dog stopped to pee and, in that moment, time stopped too. It's happening all over the place, and it's happening so easily and so spontaneously that we don't even realize what's occurring. It is important to understand what's occurring and it's important to understand the difference or we start using old paradigms for something that doesn't fit anymore. This is new.

In the old way, we had very little possibility of direct experience. Self-realization was a concept but there wasn't even a doorway to know what it meant. The only way to have some energetic, experiential taste was by reflection. It was intelligent then to go to a teacher, preferably to someone with as different a background as you could find. Another country would be perfect. If they didn't even speak English, wonderful. If you live in a country where most people are clean-shaven, find someone with the longest beard you can. They shouldn't wear Western clothes; they should be wearing robes. Everything should look different so the projection can work properly. Because it was so hard then to find this in oneself, one had to project it out, look for it in another and say, "Ah! There is the enlightenment, over there on that gold-brocaded podium, surrounded by the flowers and cameras and lights. It's out there because it can't be here. It can't be here because I know that I'm a limited being with problems, neuroses, and limitations, so it must be over there." And that was good, because it was better to have it there than nowhere at all. Better to at least see the sun reflected in a puddle than have no sun at all.

It's not necessary to do that anymore. Let's look for a minute and see why it might be not only unnecessary but even inadvisable to do that now. When you project the source of wisdom, beauty, love and peace outside onto something else, for the projection to work properly, that something else must be as removed from you as possible—not personally available. That something else is seen drifting out of the car, onto the stage, giving a discourse and disappearing again. That's the ideal way to have a projection because it's not going to get shaken very easily. But look what happens. You can hold that for a time, but then slowly you find out that this is also a human being. I'm not just speaking theoretically. This has occurred, hasn't it? Almost every icon we project onto is sooner or later exposed. And then the same adulation, the same adoration, flips into resentment, disappointment, and feeling betrayed. We project these idealized qualities onto some icon, and soon the icon turns out to be just like us. The icon has greed. The icon wants money. The icon wants to sleep with Western women. The icon wants all these things and we become bitter. But it's too late, we've donated all our money to the cause. We've sold our souls. And the intense adoration turns into deep bitterness.

As long as we project in this way, as long as we want some kind of idealism and perfection that we can project onto, then the context of our own ordinary humanity, our own thoughts, our own simple humanness is not acceptable as a context for wakefulness. We see that the icon isn't ordinary, doesn't go shopping (most of these icons don't, someone else does it for them), doesn't do the laundry, doesn't deal with money and certainly doesn't pick up the kids from school. Then we think, "I have to do all these ordinary things, so I can't be That," because it doesn't fit the model.

But now it's 1998 and we need to change models. That's why it's so important to understand that things are changing and the models from even ten years ago don't fit anymore. If you try to use an old model (and there are still teachers floating around that live that old paradigm), it's going to postpone wakefulness. This is happening these days. The realization is there, but the context in which one expects the realization to happen is different because we're used to these old models. We're used to someone who is not living an ordinary Western life, so we reject our own wakefulness because it doesn't look the way it's "supposed" to look. For this reason it's important to reevaluate—to see the possibility of wakefulness while doing the dishes, to see the possibility of wakefulness in the midst of the ordinariness of human relationships, to see the possibility of wakefulness in the midst of ordinary thoughts.

If you have a job and you deal with money, and deadlines, and employees, you will experience the mental symptoms that go along with that. When the deadline comes close, if things are not ready you will experience some sort of stress, wakeful or not wakeful. It's natural. Could we accept that? Could we accept that these things are part of human life, realized or not?

If we can accept that, if we can relax this need to project and idealize and create something superhuman on a podium, we can have planetary awakening—but only if we give up projecting. We can have millions of people waking up, but only if we are willing to give up these childish dreams of a superman or a superwoman. Do you see this? As long as we go on projecting That, we must inevitably keep ourselves in the identity of the seeker, still asking questions, still looking, because we never fit the model of the "Awakened One." You can only have a few people not doing the laundry, not working, not doing the shopping, not picking up the kids. You can only have a few people like that, the rest have to chip in and help. Someone has to take care of ordinary life. So it is important, in the name of what is trying to burst through now, to see that the way we have treated wakefulness is a kind of fantasy, and to let it go. What would it be like if we really let it go? What would it be like if we could meet together as friends and see that the one facilitating the meeting is just like you, no different from you, and just happens to be in a different role? You are good at gardening or house building or lecturing at the university and someone else is good at running a kind of spiritual David Letterman show—just a different role. The attainment is no different. The Consciousness is no different. The being That is no different. What would it be like if we could meet and abandon all hierarchy, abandon all higher and lower, just let it go? What would it be like if we could see our own lives NOW as the perfect soil for wakefulness to flourish?

The difference is simply in the seeking. There is a difference between what might be called dropping out of school and graduating from school. They look a little bit the same. If you drop out, that means you don't go to school anymore. If you graduate you also don't go to school anymore, but it feels very different to drop out than it does to graduate. Because dropping out is incomplete. Dropping out somehow has the flavor of giving up. You drop out of school and there's the feeling of never having quite finished it. Graduating means it's done. Graduating means "I'm finished." It's a very different feeling, isn't it?

To abandon seeking doesn't mean to drop out, incomplete. It doesn't mean, "Okay, I give up, but I never got it." That's dropping out. Graduating means, "Now I see that what I am seeking I already have." The seeking was just postponing the relaxing. It doesn't mean we don't go to Satsang anymore. It doesn't mean that we give up our dedication to Truth. It means that we come to Satsang like this—not seeking, not questioning, but overflowing with love. This is the true meaning of Satsang—to come, not as a seeker, but to come and celebrate the finding. And to be willing to say, "I have graduated, I am through. And I am an ordinary human being." This takes courage—to live an ordinary life, to be willing to embrace an ordinary life and to rest in the knowledge "I am done, I am cooked through and through. I have graduated and I have abandoned seeking God forever." This is worthy of prostration. There are many right here in this room who have had the courage to remain ordinary and yet give up the infantile tendencies that we all have to want to project this somewhere else. Look around, this is where our prostration needs to be. Now, as human beings we're maturing, and we're seeing that projection is no longer needed.

Let's look a little deeper at the consequences of the old paradigm, because when we project out and say, "Okay, awakening looks like this idealized life style," we inevitably, by implication, have a judgment of ordinariness. We inevitably, by implication, reject ordinary life. We reject our own ordinariness and then we reject ordinariness when we see it around us, because it doesn't have the glamour. We all know this from our experience of romantic love. When you were a teenager you probably had the experience of falling in love—and falling is the operative word here—with some romantic ideal. So when you're a teenager either you find some rock star on TV or someone at high school and, "ahh"—idealize. This we call love, but it's a very shallow kind of love because the rock star has only to sneeze and we're disillusioned. The high school sweetheart has only to get irritable and we're immediately disappointed because we were in love with an ideal. It's the same thing we've done with spiritual teachers; we were in love with a romantic ideal.

When we drop the projection, when we let go of expecting the one speaking to be perfect, what remains? We open to the possibility of real love, which can embrace ordinary human life, ordinary human stresses, ordinary human conditions, and still be love. This is spiritual maturity. This is where the essence becomes real. We start off with the question, "Who am I?" That's like Spiritual Awakening 101. It's where Ramana Maharshi's teaching begins. We discover, if we really give our attention to the question, that there's absolutely nothing there. But that's only the beginning of the discovery. From that nothing we can look into the eyes of incarnation and see the same nothing, and recognize in that awesome moment out of time that it's the same nothing looking at itself. That is real love. That is the love that can include everything, that can remain steady no matter what the context. It is completely different from the love that needs to project and idealize and that is disappointed by human frailty. It's a love that remains steady no matter if there's weakness or strength. I don't know if you're familiar with Byron Katie. Do you know who she is? She's a teacher. Before her awakening she went into a state of what could be called madness, for seven years. She was unable to do very much at all. She was very depressed and unable to function in the world. During that time she was supported by her husband, who never gave up on her. He stayed right by her side, although she was basically dysfunctional. Let me read to you about this man, Paul.

"Paul wanted to take her home immediately. She was ill. During the seven years that preceded her awakening, Katie had fallen more and more deeply into a depressive state, and Paul had taken on the service of care. He did whatever he could to carry her, to carry the family, to carry their business through. He loved them all. Paul tells me, 'When you love someone, you love them, that's all. It doesn't matter if they're fat or thin, sane or insane, sick or well, you just love them—and it goes beyond all those things.' He carried a weight not made for any human being. It wasn't his love that was so heavy. Love kept him alive. Love kept them all alive. Love is a free gift and frees the one who gives as well as the one who receives. The burden Paul carried was the requirement he placed upon himself to save them all and to keep Katie alive."

I wanted to read you that because it's really the kind of love that Satsang is about. It may begin with awakening, it may begin with the question "Who am I?" because unless That is awakened, this love cannot even begin to grow. But "Who am I?" is just a beginning; nothingness is just a beginning. Don't stop with that. Out of nothingness grows love. In this love we are all beginners, always. In this love human form and human incarnation have their justification. All the difficulties we've been through, all the struggles, are justified by this kind of love which blossoms only in the soil of wakefulness.

This is a gathering in the name of love. The trance of separation must first be broken before love can begin to reveal itself. Breaking the trance of separation in and of itself is nothing much. The preoccupation is still with "my" freedom, "my" enlightenment, "my" spiritual state—which is still very self-absorbed. Once you break beyond that into the mystery of "Who is this I look at? What is this creation before me?" then love begins, love has no end, and in that love everything makes sense. In that love there is real fulfillment. In the name of that love, in the name of this gathering, look and see what remains to obscure that. Once the habits of idealizing perfection are abandoned then real perfection can show up.

Did you ever read the book by Stephen Levine and his wife, called *Embracing the Beloved*? If you haven't read it, I would suggest that it's an absolute requirement for being human. It's like the bible on love. It's written from such a place of humility, mercy and compassion. It's really a book about how marriage and relationship can become a context for real love—not for needy love, but for real love. There is a sentence in there that has been etched into my heart like a knife in stone. He says, "Real love looks at the beloved and says, 'This person may not be perfect, but they're perfect for me.'" This is the fruit of wakefulness. Once the question "Who am I?" is asked and nothing comes, then there is a maturing, and the whole interest in being awake disappears. It is eclipsed by a love that says, "This which is before me may not be perfect according to some idealized scale, but it's perfect for me." In that seeing the whole purpose of creation is justified.

All projection, whether it is positive or negative, must be abandoned in the name of love. Love says: "You are beautiful, just like me; you are insecure, just like me; you are angry, just like me." Love sees you as you are in your strength and your weakness and says, "You are just like me." Projection says: "You are wise, unlike me; you are loving and compassionate, unlike me." And then it turns to someone else and says: "You are mean, unlike me; you are irresponsible, unlike me." It's so simple when we see it. You can dissolve judgment with one little phrase: "just like me." Just add that to everything you say about anyone — "just like me" — and projection dissolves.

Asking the question, "Who am I?" and recognizing there is nothing there is easy. To ask a question and not find any answer is pretty easy. And that brings, at least momentarily, an awakening. Dissolving the habits that create separation is also easy, but not habitual and requires some patience. Asking "Who am I?" and recognizing "Whoops! There's nothing there. Whoopee, I'm enlightened!" is just the beginning course, Spiritual Awakening 101. Then what follows is having the maturity, the courage and the honesty to face the mountain of habits that have supported duality, and to let each be dissolved. There are many — not all, but many — who in the name of *Advaita* or non-duality go for the easy part, "Who am I? Nobody there! Whoopee, I'm awake!" and never do the rest, which is the undoing. They never find the willingness to stand steady and face all the old habits to let them be dissolved or to face all the unlove that has accumulated. I'm not speaking philosophically; I'm speaking completely pragmatically.

This demonstrates some schism between what is being said and heard and what is being lived. This demonstrates that when there is the waking up to one's true nature there must also be the willingness to stand steady and face all of the old demons that created duality. Some say that everything is extinguished in this initial recognition. I say, "Good luck!" I'm just being pragmatic. Asking the question and having this recognition that is called awakening is very easy and is kind of overrated a bit these days. People have a glimpse and then think, "I am awakened. Now everything is done." Not true. Now there comes the challenge to embody That, which may take the rest of one's life. Now must come the complete surrender to That, the absolute prostration to the Truth that has been seen.

35

Nowhere to Go

Everything that feels abhorrent to the heart
Occurs in the name of separation.
To overlook the magnificence of your true nature
Is to wander in unnecessary suffering,
Driven by endless desire.

There have been all kinds of
Mythological accounts of Hell—
Roaring fires,
Delicious food just out of reach—
It's all in Dante.

I tell you, you don't have to look far
To find Hell.
Being driven by desire for that which is not
And overlooking that which is—
That is Hell.
Wanting to be with one who is absent
And overlooking the one you're with—
That is Hell.

To overlook the Mystery of your Self
Is to live in unnecessary suffering.
To relax into the great Mystery
In the midst of ordinary life
Is immediately Heaven.
You don't need to die and go anywhere—
Right here there is perfection.

36

In the Fire

This is an age of fully embodied awakening,
The shining of the Self into everyday life.

Relationship becomes a vehicle of Self reaching Self.
Ordinary human life becomes a reflection of Oneness.

This is courageous *dharma*,
Acknowledging wakefulness
And remaining in the fire of embodiment.

37

Go Out and Boogie

When I'm in Satsang, I feel free and empty, but in my life I easily get identified.

When you go to the movies,
First you pay for your ticket.
You give some energy
To have an experience of a story.
You sit down in a dark room
Because you've paid for and chosen
A temporary experience of identification.
Tremendous energy
Has gone into creating that
For your entertainment.

If you sit in a movie theater
Obsessed with the idea
"This is just a movie;
I'm in a movie theater.
This is just flickering images
On a white screen.
I will not get identified."
You won't have any fun!
You may stay theoretically free,
But so what?
What is the point of going to the movies
Just so you can be free?
You have to dance a little bit
With why you are there.

How About Now?

You have been empty,
Free, unborn, undying,
Limitlessness Consciousness eternally.
Before anything ever happened,
You were That.
When it's all said and done,
When the whole circus is packed up and put away,
You'll still be That.
But within That there was a choice made
by Consciousness itself
(Which is you),
To create diversity,
To have creation.

People get confused.
They start quoting Indian philosophy,
Which is not properly understood or digested,
And say that the whole purpose of creation
Is to have this emptiness.
It's ridiculous.
There was emptiness forever,
Before creation.
Why do you need creation to have emptiness?
There has been a choice made
By Consciousness
To incarnate
And have an experience of diversity.
Enjoy it!
Why fight it?
Inherent in your question
Is putting this empty, free, floating state
Above identification.
But you're here to get involved
And to get your feet dirty.

You don't have to do anything.
It's already taken care of—
Just relax.
You are already spacious and empty;
You always were.
An impulse of Divine will has arisen
From out of your own Self
To go out and boogie,
To be formlessness in form.
That is what you are here for.
Now Dance—with abandon!

38

Let Go

The one who speaks these words
You find in your own Heart
As your Heart.
This is the teaching:
To let go of all teaching.

Let go of all that has been heard,
All that has been said,
And see what's left.

What remains is Ocean,
Which is neither awake nor unawake.
It is beyond all duality.

You have always been That,
From long before the body took form.
Who you are will always be That,
Long after the body has ceased to be.

The teaching is not to become awakened
Or enlightened.
The teaching is to give up such nonsense.
Surrender.

Do not fulfill the search
But give up the search.
Abandon seeking for That
Which was never lost.

39

We Meet as Beginners

Longing must be surrendered to, respected. You can't say anything about it. You don't even know what you're longing for or who is longing. There is just longing.

It tries to find objects — the guru, Krishna, a lover — something it can pour itself into. Ultimately, all those objects are washed away in the longing for Love to relax more and more deeply into itself.

It starts with emptiness. That's the source.
It ends in Love. That's the flowering.

So never mind what anyone says to you. When you feel the longing of your heart, let that longing itself be your teacher.

Obey it. Surrender to it. Let it take over everything. In this we meet as beginners. Become like a child. You cannot be anything but a beginner in the realm of Love.

It's always one on one. It brings you to your knees endlessly in humility.

Where is the end of Love? Where can you say, "Ah, now I have one hundred percent of Love"? You always feel like you are at the beginning; there is always infinitely more to explore.

Travel to what you thought was the edge. Find out you are always just at the beginning.

40

No Preferences

*W*hen you are with other people do you experience that you are alone, in a sense, or do you experience them as others? Or does it flip-flop between the two?

All of the above and more, just like you. Just now, in this moment here, who are you meeting? What does your heart say?

I am meeting myself.

You have the realization, "I am meeting my Self," and simultaneously there is the recognition, "This form I am meeting looks and sounds different from me." There is the recognition of difference and sameness at the same time. To linear thought, that seems contradictory. But this is the play.

In certain dimensions I see my Self. Yet it is not always literally like that, or it would take all the fun out of diversity. If you say to yourself, "I want more of seeing my Self everywhere," what is implicitly created as your reality?

That I don't have that.

Wanting it creates its lack. Could you just relax into the inevitability that both are absolutely true? It is your Self everywhere, and there is diversity. There is a way to rest in these moments of profound sameness and moments of perceiving great difference. This is Freedom.

What you have been describing so far is a spiritual experience. If you become attracted to one end of that polarity rather than the other, you are caught in desire. It is desire that keeps you from Freedom, not lack of these spiritual experiences. Spiritual experiences come and go, but seeing that sameness and diversity are both contained in something greater than both of them is called Freedom. It is called Truth.

There is always the ocean with waves moving within it. If you try to keep away the waves of diversity, you are caught in desire. If you welcome all diversity, you relax in freedom, which has no preferences.

This is your own heart's wisdom.

41

Surrender

*M*y name is Ann. I am a small businessperson and have a lot of people depending on me. I am being pushed to change, and I don't know how to change.

Running your own business does have its rough and smooth times. You have independence. Working for a big corporation can be another kind of burden.

What kind of business are you running?

A roll-in shop, a car wash and quick lube.

Well, that sounds like a pretty complete outfit: "Take Care of All Your Needs in One Stop." Let me ask you something. When Ann is held in compassion, she is doing the best she can, isn't she? She is lubing and she is washing. She's not trying to cheat anybody and she is giving good service.

Yes.

So when you are being held in compassion in this way, who is embracing you? Who is holding Ann when she is embraced like this? What is found?

I don't know.

And yet Ann is being embraced, isn't she? She is being held by "I Don't Know." Are the employees being held by "I Don't Know" too? This business, could you give it to "I Don't Know" to run? The One who embraces Ann and the employees—could the business be signed over to That?

Yes.

This signing over, obviously, you can't do with an attorney because you don't know who you are signing it over to. Nevertheless, when you transfer ownership of a business, it needs some kind of paperwork, some kind of symbol.

Could you go out tomorrow and find some symbol, some icon, something beautiful that you could put on your desk to symbolize the transfer of ownership from Ann to the One who embraces all beings? Could you do that? You won't know exactly what it represents. You will just have the icon there, and every time you feel stressed, you will look at the icon and think, "Oh, why am I worried? I have handed over this business to someone else." Could you do that, Ann?

The relaxing of habits and control in the name of this handing over may take a little time. So be patient. If anxiety arises, look at the symbol on your desk and remind yourself, "I am a faithful employee. I am not slacking off. I am showing up for work but I have given up control."

Giving up control does not mean that you are being irresponsible. You are going to be a faithful manager. Maybe you will work very hard for "I Don't Know." But everything is handed over to "I Don't Know," the One who cradles Ann. Ultimately, "I Don't Know" is Who You Are, but in moments of identification, "I Don't Know" will seem like a benevolent mother. That's okay too, because it works. This is Business Management 101 for the 21st Century.

We have the fear that if we give up, things will stop happening and there will be chaos. But quite the opposite is revealed. When you hand something over, you are declaring, "I'm out of here. I take my hands off the steering wheel. It's your show now." You can do that with your business. You will still work, but you will receive your instructions from the Boss. The instructions will come so clearly that they will just translate immediately into impulse and action, without thought intervening. The instruction comes and — voom — it just happens through you. That's surrender.

We are all beginners, Ann. You lube and wash cars. That is the role that the Self, the Truth, has given Ann. I sit in rooms and talk. It is just a different role. We are all beginners, we human forms. We are all just experimenting with the embodiment of Truth.

42

The Mirror

This is not about a teacher
Or getting something from a teacher.

The teacher points you back to yourself
Until you recognize who you are.

Then the teacher is everywhere.

It is all a mirror of your true Self.
It is only in resting in your true Self
That the teaching is fulfilled.

In a strange way,
The only way to do justice to a teacher
Is to walk away

Because if you cling to the teacher
You are not hearing the teaching.

The teacher is telling you to look into yourself,
To become your own light.

Then teacher and student merge and become friends.

43

Doubt is a Thought

I was wondering if you could talk a little bit about doubt? My experience is that when I'm in Satsang it's real easy, and then sometimes when I'm alone or in other contexts there is doubt that arises in the face of that incredible happiness. It says, "You must be nuts."

What is that? "You must be nuts." What is it?

It's a thought.

Yes, it's a thought. What else does doubt say?

This is silly.

What is that?

Four more words. This is really silly.

"This is really silly." What is that?

Another thought.

Now try this: "You are a great enlightened being." What's that?

Another thought.

Now we're no longer in the doubt category, we're in the "I got it" category. "You must be nuts." "You are a great enlightened being." What difference does it make? Two thoughts. Then we had, "This is silly." We could try, "This is very profound." Just two more thoughts, you see.

When a thought comes that says, "This is very silly," or when a thought comes that says, "This is truly profound, great non-dual *Advaita*," is there a choice or a decision or an effort prior to the thought arising to have a thought?

No.

It doesn't require any premeditation. Where did thought come from? Suddenly, there's a thought—zoom—there's another one. They arise on their own. They're self-originating.

Other than the thought, is there anything to be found called a "thinker" creating thoughts?

No.

They just arise out of nowhere. Did you ever drink soda drinks in a glass? Have you ever wondered where the bubbles come from? As a child I used to wonder about that. You watch, and out of nowhere, suddenly there's a bubble. Where did it come from? I used to look under the table. I had a lot of fantasies about that when I was a child—what is the source of the bubbles? In fact, I think you could write a hitch-hikers-guide-to-the-galaxy-style book around that—where do the bubbles come from in soda drinks? They just appear. No source—they just arise out of nowhere.

Since thought arises on its own anyway and there's no decision to have it or not, is there anything you can do about it?

No.

All you can do is add another layer of thought called "That's not an okay thought," but that's just more thought too. Since it's arising anyway and there's no choice about it, you might as well let it be because it's going to happen anyway.

Now, in just letting it be, if the interest is no longer paid so much to the content of thought, what difference does it make if there is a so-called doubting thought or a so-called enlightened thought? Does it make any difference? Does it actually make any difference to this moment? Try it consciously. Go ahead now and think this thought deliberately: "This is complete rubbish."

Okay.

Now try thinking this thought: "I love this guy; this is the best evening of my life." Does it make any difference to this moment?

No, but what's more convincing to me are the feelings that appear from nowhere.

Okay, so do one thing. Just stay here with your eyes and have the thought, "This is really stupid" and think it to the point that it actually generates a feeling. But stay present with your eyes.

Good. Now try another one. Look at me with your eyes and just for a moment have the feeling that we are completely in love.

Okay, now tell me, as those thoughts drift on by, did either one make any difference to what's here?

Not really, no.

There is really only one choice, and it's the only choice that one gets to make in this moment. The choice is whether to listen to the unreal or not to listen. You can't prevent these thoughts from arising. They will actually subside slowly as less attention is paid to them. There is only one choice, which is whether to fixate on them or not. The only way to not fixate on them is to return the attention to the real, to that which experiences all thought. Then doubts or great enlightened insights are exactly the same. It makes no difference, absolutely no difference at all.

"I am enlightened" is just another thought.

What about a feeling?

It is the same thing when a feeling state comes. Do you decide, "Okay, I think I'm going to have some sadness now?" Is that how it is? Doesn't an event just occur and sadness arises? You can try to repress it but it's going to get you anyway. Can't that also be welcomed?

What is left then if all ideas of what should and shouldn't be are abandoned?

Quiet.

Quiet, yes. That quiet, does it require particular kinds of thoughts in order to be quiet?

No

Does it require an absence of thought to be quiet?

No.

It's a quiet that has no opposite. It's a quiet that includes noise. And that's who you are. It's not an experience; it's not a state. It is who you are all the time. You have never been other than That, and you will never be other than That. And about that there is no choice. It's the only item on the menu, and the waiter will bring it whether you order it or not.

So now what's left?

Quiet and happiness.

Yes, quiet and happiness, which is always there — not an attainment, not an experience and not a state. This happiness that you speak of, could it also include misery?

Yes!!

It is a happiness that has no opposite, a happiness that includes everything. You could call that acceptance. You could call that compassion. It's the abandonment of all resistance to life.

This is the invitation right now. It can't be postponed. It's either now or it's not. There's no tomorrow in this. "Tomorrow" is just a way of saying no. This is the invitation. This is neither enlightenment nor unenlightenment; this is neither free nor bound. This is the inevitable Truth.

44

Contradictions Are Embraced by the Heart

I heard you speak last night, and now you seem to be saying the opposite. Yet both opposites seem true.

Whatever one says in language,
the opposite is also true.
Including this statement!!
Truth is vast—
It contains everything.
There is no contradiction.

In Satsang
Speaking does not need effort.
It happens.
That speaks as it needs to speak.
And it's full of contradiction.
To thought it seems like contradiction;
To the Heart it's just as it is
And it's all true.

Yes, yesterday you pointed out that thought is occurring anyway, and it's all perfect, all happening in Consciousness. Today, you are pointing out the danger of following thought. And both are true.

There is no way to escape Presence.
Thinking about childhood with regret
Is happening in Presence.
Thinking about the future with great anxiety

How About Now?

Is also occurring in Presence.
And at the same time,
There is a calling in this gathering to recognize,
Perhaps just for a moment,
The difference between what is real
And what is imaginary,
To recognize the way that there has been
An addiction to the imaginary.
Perhaps just for a moment
That recognition is needed,
And then it blossoms.
People read that or hear that or grasp that
"Oh well, it's all just perfect,"
And it becomes complacency.
Once the context in which all that is occurring
Has been recognized,
Then everything is recognized as perfect.
Until the context has been recognized,
There is only resistance and identification.

Someone comes, really caught
In profound anxiety about the future.
Their body is wrapped in that anxiety.
Just to tell them,
"Well, the anxiety is perfect; it's all happening in the now,"
In a philosophical sense is true
And in an absolute sense is true,
But it doesn't serve form.
If someone is living in nostalgia, regret, mourning of some kind,
To tell them, "The mourning and the regret
And the trying to change the past in the mind
Is all perfect. It's happening in the now,"
Is absolutely true, but it doesn't serve form.
If there can be the compassion to bring attention
To this moment,
To bring attention and hold attention to this moment

Just long enough that attention falls in love with this moment,
Then comes the recognition,
"Ah, this past that has been haunting me is a thought."
Now there has been an awakening
To the difference between real experience
And the thought about it.

It's just a shift of gestalt.
Once the recognition comes
That this future I'm worrying about isn't the real thing —
It's a thought that will never occur —
Then comes relaxation;
Those thoughts are welcome but they make no difference.
People come with longing in the heart for a deeper recognition.

Buddha lived this contradiction.
One of his buddies said to him,
"What was it that happened to you under the *bodhi* tree
when you attained supreme, eternal enlightenment?"
Buddha replied, "Absolutely nothing happened.
That is why it is called supreme, eternal enlightenment —
Nothing happened."
And yet that nothing which never happened
Makes all the difference in the world.

45

Divine Mother

I don't know how to make decisions. I really want to let go and step beyond thought, as you suggest, but there are decisions that must be made in life that involve thought and responsibility.

I'm going to ask you something, and you just answer me innocently, intuitively. Do you have the first clue as to what is going on? Do you have any idea of what to do?

Well yes, I have a lot of ideas of what to do.

But do any of them seem very reliable?

No, it feels like grasping in the dark

Right. So you feel pretty lost, don't you? You haven't got the first clue of what to do. That's okay. Join the club.

And these thoughts and all this stuff—would you know how to switch them off, even if you wanted to?

No.

Even though you don't know what to do, even though you feel lost, and even though things seem a little out of control, nevertheless, when was the last time you didn't eat for a day for lack of food? When was the last time you didn't have a roof over your head?

Those things are not the problem.

So you are taken care of.

It seems like it takes a lot of effort though.

Yes, and is the effort getting you anywhere?

Well, if I stop doing the effort then things slide away. I just don't do them. And then I forget things and everything just gets worse.

Let's come back a minute to keep it simple. Has your physical survival been in any real danger at all?

At a basic level, no.

All right. So let's face it. The reality, whether you like it or not, is that you don't really know what to do. You feel kind of lost, which is natural. Even though you feel kind of lost, does it seem like something is causing life to carry on anyway?

Sometimes.

Sometimes. You see, when you stop efforting, then you can recognize that. What I want to suggest to you is this: see if you can feel, just for a moment, the benevolence in life, the protection in life. It doesn't take much. Just review your life and think about all the things that have happened.

Many blessings.

Yes, many blessings. Did they come through effort or did they come as blessings?

It seemed to be a combination of putting something out and having it bear fruit.

Here's what I suggest you do. Every time you start to feel lost and out of control and you don't know what to do, just hand it all over to the Divine Mother. Just bow to her. She takes care of the universe. Bow to her and say, "I don't have a clue, Ma. Everything I try to do doesn't work out the way that I thought it would, so you take over." You tell her to take over, and then prostrate to her.

This is a little trick, you see, because the one you are prostrating to is who you really are when you are quiet. When you are quiet, you are the Divine Mother. But if you're caught up in the dream of not being the Divine Mother, put her outside yourself and bow to her. You will end up in the same place that inquiry takes you to. It's just two different routes to the same glorious destination. One way is to look back and ask, "Who Am I?" and you see that you are Awareness, which is the Divine Mother. But if you feel churned up and it's too difficult to do that, just put her outside and say, "Ma, I have no idea what I'm doing. I'm lost. You take over. I put myself in your hands and whatever you decide, I'll follow." It will become obvious then what to do. The right action will simply reveal itself in a very natural way.

It's all the same: prostrating to the Divine Mother, handing your life over, or inquiring, "Who am I?" It's all the same.

"Who am I?" doesn't seem to work too well with me.

It doesn't matter; you can play with both. Try it now. Turn to Ma and say, "Ma, I give you my life. I remove my hands from the steering wheel. It's up to you now."

You mean right now?

Yes.

"Divine Mother, I surrender my life to you, to your wisdom and your care."

And now just let yourself be quiet and feel her response.

There's quite a relaxation.

Yes, that's right. Hand your life over, and then get quiet and wait. She will answer you—sometimes with a word, sometimes just with a feeling. The feeling of relaxation is as though she is saying to you, "Be still. Relax. Be still."

You can say to her, "Ma, I'm identified with my thoughts, please help me. I feel inadequate and I don't know what to do. I don't think I can do it right. Whatever you say to do, I will do it." Hand it all over and get quiet. Try that for a few days and then come again and report.

The truth is, as far as the person you've taken yourself to be, you can't do it right. You are not capable of doing it right, ever.

I know. The one I take myself to be thinks she's the only one on the planet out of six billion people who's not going to make it.

So you just say, "Ma, I can't do it right." Then tell her, "Since I can't do it right, Ma, you take over." Just try it. Every time this arises, just hand it all over and you'll see. This kind of prayer is always answered. If you ask for a new red truck, you may not get it. If you ask for the winning lottery numbers, you may not get them. If you just say, "Thy will be done," it never fails.

I've been asking to be shown my true nature.

So try this, between now and next Satsang. Just make it your constant song.

Whether through inquiry or devotion, either one will bring you back to your Self. The more you surrender to the Divine Mother, the more you give up the notion of an individual identity. And then what's left is the Mother—which is universal awareness, which is love, you see. It's all the same; it doesn't matter.

46

The Birth of Love

When the recognition of No One there
Can meet the same Nothing
In an apparent other,
This is the birth of Love;
This is the pinnacle of creation.

Explore just now and see:
Who is looking back at you?

The same "my Self" is everywhere!
All manifestation reveals
There is no otherness anywhere.

47

Embrace Pain

I wonder sometimes how to look at pain. How can we look at those moments when we are experiencing discomfort so that we don't become bound by pain and identify with distress?

Is there pain now?

On some level, yes.

So, on some level there is discomfort. Would you say there is some underlying pain, as well?

Yes, sort of an unresolved residue.

Let's sit with this for a second. Do you mind if we just explore this pain together for a moment?

Okay.

Now this residue of pain, which is unresolved and is lingering in some way right now, is it welcome or unwelcome?

It is unwelcome.

Tell me, do you have children?

No, but I work with children.

What ages are they?

They range from four to ten years old.

Have you noticed what happens if a child is unhappy and tries to get your attention, but in some way you push the child away?

Yes, the child becomes more intense.

Exactly. Then what happens?

They start to cry.

They become more insistent, don't they? A child may even become violent, may drop and break something or hit another child, in an attempt to get your attention.

On the other hand, if the child is unhappy, and you turn immediately to the child and bring him or her to your heart, what happens?

The crying usually stops. There is peace.

Now, with regard to this pain, what do you think is the origin of it?

The feeling of being separate.

And where does the origin of separation come from?

Feeling cut off from the source.

Yes, and where did feeling cut off from the source originate?

From falling asleep.

Okay, and what is the origin of falling asleep?

Well, I guess it's being born into physical reality.

Now, do you think it is the physical reality that has caused separation or the relationship to reality that has created a sense of disconnection?

The relationship to reality.

And what is the source of this relationship to reality?

Thought.

Good, good. And what is the origin of thought?

It comes from me.

So perhaps this pain is like your child. The pain has arisen from within you. It's not from outside. It's your child, like a child you talk to.

Then, in the same way, if you push the pain away, just like the child...

Distress comes up in different forms. The pain takes on different faces.

Beautiful. But just for a moment, there is another way to experience it. With your breath, could you just welcome it? Simply say, "Ah, come." In the same manner you might say it to a child. Just say, "Come."

Can you hold it more closely? Yes! How is it now?

It's different.

Yes, isn't it? Could you embrace it more, maybe even cuddle it?

I could work on it.

Does it take work to cuddle?

How About Now?

It's just that this is a new way of looking at it and experiencing it.

I understand. That's all right. Well, just for the fun of it then, try opening your heart and saying to the pain, "Come here. Come, sweetheart. I'm sorry I pushed you away."

How is it now?

It's different. It changes.

And now?

Well it takes on a different shape because it's being loved.

Wonderful. All right, now it is being loved. So there is the pain and the feeling of embracing the pain. Pain is arising and falling, and it is being embraced. It is being loved.

Let's do one little thing more. We've been working with the pain, right? Now, let's shift the attention from the pain to that which is experiencing the pain. Turn your awareness to That which is loving the pain.

What is loving the pain? Look back into your Self and find out. Who is embracing the pain?

Me.

Very nice. "Me." Now look into "me" and turn the attention back into what you call "me."

Well, it feels bigger than me.

Yes, bigger. Now find the limits to This that is experiencing the pain. Where are the limits, the edges of the experiencer?

There don't seem to be any.

Ah, wonderful! No limits! The pain is being embraced by That which has no edges and no limits. Now just in this moment, which is more interesting, the pain or the limitlessness?

Oh, the limitlessness.

Beautiful. But the pain does have limits, doesn't it? It's fleeting. It comes, and it goes.

The pain seems to be informative. It's important.

Ah, that's the crux, you see. When there is more interest in pain and what information it might have than about being limitless, there is suffering. This shift in perception is optional.

So you're saying that I'm more interested in suffering than I am in being limitless if I'm continually experiencing pain? Is that accurate?

Let's find out. Let's find out right now. Stay here. Put the attention on the pain, the information the pain may have and, therefore, follow the story of the pain. Who did what to whom? How does that feel?

Well, it's not very comfortable.

So when the interest is in the story that the pain wants to tell, there is suffering. But we have also discovered tonight that the pain is being experienced and can be loved by that which is limitless. When you relax back into the limitlessness, which is experiencing the pain in the moment, then there is love.

That's wonderful.

Now, tell me, that option to follow the pain or to follow the limitlessness, what could take away that choice? What experience might arise that could take away the possibility of being limitless?

How About Now?

Well, falling asleep and assuming that this kind of understanding is not an option.

When you say "falling asleep," what is it that falls asleep?

The "I" would forget that seeing limitlessness is an option.

Who forgets?

Okay, I see! There is no forgetting.

You know, it sounds strange, but it is actually true. Buddha said the same thing. He said that in the awakening there was the recognition that he had never been asleep. It was an illusion. This falling asleep and forgetting is a fallacy. It never actually happens. There is no falling asleep in Consciousness, don't you see? Falling asleep happens to someone who doesn't exist. There is just this option, which is a choice really, taken by no one. The decision is for attention to follow a story of woe, which then becomes a personal life. And pain creates pain. Have you noticed? The distressing lack of conclusion to last week's pain becomes the creation of situations today that cause the sense of more affliction. Live in unresolved pain and you create more pain. You see, this that has been revealed tonight is always accessible. I can testify that in the midst of all kinds of human dilemmas, this is available.

You can live in constant peace. It may not look that way to others because when challenges arise, the body may fall out of balance. We may become tired or sick. But this which is experiencing disruption never leaves peace, never strays from stillness. Consciously knowing that you are limitlessness itself is what begins to inform and guide the movements of your life.

There's no need to take my word for it. You have already

experienced a taste of it tonight and it will just naturally begin to show itself more and more clearly in unexpected ways.

That's beautiful. Thank you.

48

Seeds of Love

How can I know the interconnectedness of everything? I can understand it intellectually but haven't yet experienced it.

The concept of
Interconnectedness among all beings
Is just a concept,
And as a concept it is plastic food.
It cannot nourish you at all
As a concept.
In fact,
Once you've got plastic food on your plate,
It's taking up space where real food could be.
Better to reject the concept
And instead, find out who or what it is,
Just now,
Who is aware of the concept
And aware of these words.
Genuinely,
Not conceptually,
Ask yourself,
Just now,
In this moment,
"Who Am I?
Who is here?
Who is aware of thought?"
And what do you find?

(Silence)

Okay. Good.
Although the answer is silent,
Just put some code name on it
So we can speak.

The Self.

This which you're calling the Self,
Does it have any dimensions to it
When you look into yourself?

No.

Does it have any history?
Does it have any creation date stamped on it?

No.

Could it be destroyed?

No.

This is direct experience, isn't it?
This is steaming hot food
Fresh from the kitchen,
Isn't that right?
This is nothing you've read about;
This is direct experience right now.
Is that true?

Yes.

Straight from the kitchen.
Good.
Now do one thing:
Just stay absolutely resting as That —

How About Now?

Limitless,
Outside of time,
Unborn,
Uncreated,
Present—
And look here at the eyes of this form,
Not at the form of Arjuna
But through the form of Arjuna.
Find out who is looking back at you.
Let yourself recognize, not the form,
But the one looking through the form.
What is that?

Stay here.
Don't touch concepts;
Stay here.
From That which you recognize yourself to be—
Limitless,
Unborn,
Undying,
Vast,
Free,
Empty—
Now recognize who "the other" is.
What is discovered?
Now speak.
What do you see?
Let your heart answer.

(Hesitating) It seems to be me.

Beautiful! "It seems to be me."
This is not poetry;
This is literally true.
This is the actual truth.

This is love.
This is the seed of love.
If that sameness
Is allowed to reveal itself,
This becomes the tree of love,
This becomes the orchard of love,
This becomes the forest of love,
And it begins with this seed here:
Sameness.
This is not the concept
Of the interconnectedness of all things,
This is the direct realization
That I am speaking with myself;
Not poetically,
Not philosophically,
But genuinely—
I speak with my Self.
I look into the eyes of my own Self.

Twenty fingers,
Two noses,
Four eyes,
And one Consciousness;
This is real food.

Now feast yourself on this.
This is nourishing.
This fulfills the very purpose of creation,
This recognition.
Seeing things this way,
Nothing is left to be desired,
Nothing is left incomplete.
The heart is full
And you can die in this recognition at peace.

How About Now?

Now one can say
With absolute meaning,
"I love you."
Now it means something to say that.
Now "I love you"
Doesn't mean,
"I want to manipulate you.
I want your approval.
I want you to overlook my insecurity
So that I will overlook yours."
It doesn't mean,
"I need you.
I want to hold onto you.
I want to possess you."
Now "I love you" means,
"I see who you are and
I see that it is myself.
And I need no more from you
Than I need from my own Self.
I have no more need to manipulate you
Than the sky has to manipulate its own self."
This is love.
Free.

Why does this separateness hang on so hard?

Habit.
Not seeing.
Go to the grocery store,
Buy your groceries,
Take them up to the check-out stand,
And then remember to look
Into the eyes of the one operating the cash register
And find out: "Who is this?"
Take the time.
Take the dedication to love

To ask:
"Who is this one now?"
And you'll see the same as you see here.

When you are involved in a business,
Look into the eyes of your client
And take the time to ask this question:
"Who is this one?"
The same will be revealed.

Your heart says "Yes,"
Doesn't it?
"Yes" to the unavoidable truth,
The undeniable truth.
Once this song is sung
Then you know it's your own song.
You can walk away whistling it to yourself.
Then you need no radio,
Throw the radio away—
Whistle, and sing, and skip, and jump.
Then what a great planet this becomes!

49

Heartbreak

Here in Satsang I feel full and complete, but lately I have been passing through the end of a relationship and my heart feels like it has been broken.

When we try to get something from "the other,"
There must be heartbreak.
It doesn't matter if they give you what you want
Or not,
There still must be heartbreak.
If they don't give it to you,
Or if they give it and withdraw it,
Of course there's heartbreak.
But if they do give it to you,
There's an even more uncomfortable heartbreak.
You're better off getting rejected
Than getting what you thought you wanted.
If you get what you thought you wanted,
You've got this great external circumstance
But there is still a hollowness in your heart;
You still feel empty.
What a nightmare!

There is another possibility of being with people
That doesn't bring heartbreak.
Every time you're with another
In the role of caring, giving, and emanating the love that you are,
There cannot be heartbreak.
How could there be?
You are just sharing your own fullness.
Whenever we place ourselves in relationship to get love—

"I don't have love," or "I need love,"
There must be heartbreak.
You simply have to pass through that again and again and again.
You have to eat sour apples enough times that finally,
When you go to the grocery store
They just don't look appealing anymore.
Stop looking to get love
And relax into being love itself.
Be alive with urgent love
And say goodbye to heartbreak.

50

Welcome Everything

At the moment of Awakening,
The rest of one's life
Becomes a process of discovering what has been resisted,
Then welcoming it and dissolving it.
Inevitably what has been resisted
Will be drawn into your life to be accepted.

Every day is an opportunity for constant deepening.
How can there be a final end to the embodiment of Love?
It is an endless process of breathing and oozing Limitlessness
Into form.

The key is to embrace and welcome each thing as it arises,
So that when the most devastating experience comes
You can find a way to say to yourself:

"Yes, yes, come. I'm ready.
Come, in the name of freedom.
I would rather have you come and devastate me
So that I may dissolve deeper into freedom,
Than keep you at bay and live in a prison of false security.
Come, whatever demon this is.
I welcome you."

51

The Pull of the Heart

When children grow, they pass through what are called, in psychological language, various developmental stages. It is actually quite interesting if you're a parent, to notice the bizarre nature of these developmental stages. There is the stage of being completely dependent—nursing, just holding the mother—and at that stage this is absolutely necessary, appropriate, and normal. If an eight-year-old child behaves in the same way, that's not considered healthy.

Then there's the stage where the child is just completely running on "no." This is called "the terrible twos." "Eat your dinner." "No!" "Put on your shoes." "No!" This stage is about breaking dependency and discovering independence. If the child were to say "no" as a newborn, this would not be healthy at that age. If the child is still saying "no" at forty-three, there is also a problem.

Later on, around the age of six, comes the stage of trying to please. "Can I do that for you?" "Let me do the dishes." All these stages are necessary. Then come the teenage years (which I have not yet come to enjoy with my children) when the child begins to say, "Like, who cares, man!"

Similarly, although freedom exists out of time, there are also developmental stages within the mind/body in the realization of freedom. It is worth recognizing the difference between these developmental stages because, as a mind/body, it is possible to get stuck in a stage that is no longer authentic.

Before any hint comes of something beyond ordinary life, choices in life are determined entirely by "my pleasure" and "my desire." Before you meet any Indian gurus or do any workshops the focus is basically, "I want more good stuff and I don't want pain. I want more money, more sex with more people, less income tax, more food, and less indigestion." And then (not for many, probably for less than one percent of the population), comes the dawning recognition that perhaps there might be something more to life beyond "I," "me," "mine." This is called the beginning of spiritual seeking.

In this phase of seeking for peace, most of us have been willing to do almost anything to get there. We have obeyed all kinds of dictates—chanting whatever we were told to chant, changing our diets, there are all kinds of interesting things we've done in the name of trying to get what we thought was enlightenment. If you look around the world, it's not primarily a world of people seeking freedom, is it? So this is already a rare blessing. In seeking, however, there is still this preoccupation with "I," "me," "mine"—"My freedom." Seeking is even more narcissistic and self-centered than the previous phase, isn't it? In seeking, it's "My diet," and "My posture." "What kind of thoughts am I having? Why am I having thoughts at all? Are they positive thoughts or negative thoughts? How am I doing? Is it okay?" Seeking becomes self-obsession.

I don't think anyone has ever found what they were seeking—at least I've never met anyone who suddenly got what their fantasy of enlightenment was! But for a small percentage (one percent of the one percent, perhaps) comes the recognition, "I have always been what I was seeking for. I have always been That." This is realization; this is freedom. And with respect to seeking, that is the end.

There is also a maturing that follows. Not as far as freedom goes, but as far as the mind/body there is a maturing in this freedom. The first wave is, "I got it! I'm enlightened! I'm free! Are you free? I'm free. Are you still seeking? Aww—I'm free! Let me tell you what it's like to be free! On the 23rd of September I realized the Self and now I'm free. Before that I wasn't free and now I am free." Does that sound familiar? This is the "I" that was seeking. It has a momentum, so now it grabs hold of the realization of That which doesn't change and tries to hold it as its own. This phase also comes to an end with the realization that freedom and "I" have nothing to do with each other.

There is another stage where this "I" is abandoned and the realization comes that there is really nothing to do and nowhere to go; there really is no doer anyway. There's just Consciousness, and this wave is "I'm just resting as Consciousness. Are you still 'doing?' Not me, I'm just resting as Consciousness. Nothing to do—it's all just unfolding on its own." This is another phase, a little more mature than "I got it, I got it, I got it!" Now there's no one to get anything; there's just resting and things unfold naturally.

Each of these phases in the beginning has a kind of freshness, but once it gets into a repetitive groove it gets boring. Many people comment on this. People return again and again to Satsang or to retreats or to other events and have little glimpses of silence or of peace, but they do not last. So life becomes completly concerned with how to keep these glimpses, and how to not get caught up and identified. But after a while the obsession with "me" just gets boring. One day one switches on the TV, and there is news of a hurricane in Central America, or an Earthquake in Turkey, or some other catastrophe, and then getting it and loosing it and all associated dramas pale in comparison. The attention expands to the needs of the rest of "me", to all the incarnations of the One Me.

There comes a time when even the interest in realization, even the interest in being free or not free, also subsides. "I'm free, I'm free, there's nobody there!"—how long can that be fascinating? Then, for some—and this is actually a rare thing—there comes the realization that this is all you. You're not just one small human form, there are actually more than six billion of you. Everything that's happening on this planet, even with animals, is happening to you. If there's pain anywhere, it's your pain. If there's judgment anywhere, it's your judgment. If there's violence anywhere, it's your violence. If people are fighting, it's a fight within you. This is not a sense of personal guilt ("Oh God, it's all my fault!") but an abandonment of the boundaries of where "I" ends and something or someone else begins. Then no one can say, "I am free" because there are six billion of you, and not all of You is free. One tiny little incarnation may have had a nice experience but there's plenty more of you to go. This realization that it's all me, all the same me—one mind, one heart—means that my heart is not truly at rest as long as I am still bound in some form somewhere. This realization is at the foundation of what Tibetan Buddhism and other schools of Buddhism know as the Bodhisattva vow—the vow that there will be constant service until all beings are liberated. The funny thing about the Bodhisattva vow is that it is a contradiction, because within the Bodhisattva vow is the realization that there are no beings to be liberated anywhere. In fact, it was said of Buddha that he came to the earth to liberate all beings and he could do that only because he realized there were no beings to liberate. Strange paradox, isn't it?

I mention this because for many of us it's time to move beyond preoccupation with the minute fluctuations of "my freedom." "Am I getting identified with thought? Am I getting caught up? Or am I resting? Maybe I should do another retreat, or maybe I should have a session." There comes a time when all that becomes like a hamster on one of those wheels. The very preoccupation with one's own state of consciousness is what keeps identification in place. What arises spontaneously from here is a life of service. That is the greatest secret.

In 1992 my teacher, Papaji, asked me to give Satsang. Naively, I thought I was supposed to go out and benefit other people, but the one who got the most benefit was actually the one giving the Satsangs. As soon as the body is used in service, the attention goes off this illusion of separate identity and starts to be concerned with the larger mind/body. For many of us, it's time to move beyond "my freedom." There's a pull of the heart, a call of the heart, to something bigger than "my spiritual state."

52

Benefits

What is different about your experience after being liberated? Do you find that you are able to let go of things quicker or that life is more workable? I mean, there had better be some sort of benefit. (Laughter)

Well, what I found is that when I go into a 7-ll and they have those tickets for the lottery, I know exactly what the six winning numbers are going to be, but I've decided for religious reasons not to use them. *(Laughter)* I've also discovered that my clothes never get dirty and I never go to the bathroom. But besides that… *(Laughter)*

No, you see, it's not like that. What happens in a moment, or in a sustained moment, is not attainment but realization. There is a big difference between attaining something and realizing something. Suppose you lose your glasses; so you look under the cushion, you look under your friend's cushion, you look in the car, you look everywhere and finally you give up. You sit down and— "Oh! There they are!" You didn't find the glasses through searching. You gave up and realized that they were on your nose all the time, you see?

What happened for Arjuna in 1991 was not an attainment. It didn't make Arjuna a better Arjuna. It was a realization that the search was futile. It was a realization that what Arjuna was looking for was what he already was. Consciousness, the One seeing through Arjuna, which is the One seeing through all beings—is already free. The personality, Arjuna, is a hopeless case. There's nothing you can do about him.

I can probably relate to that. (Laughter)

Now, there is a little proviso to this, okay? I don't want to completely flush all self-improvement down the toilet. That's not necessary. After realizing that you are Consciousness and Consciousness is pure and perfect, you still need to change the oil in your car every 3,000 miles. If you don't change the oil, it gets dirty. It doesn't mean you don't have to pay income tax anymore. If you don't pay it, you get in trouble. It doesn't mean a lot of things. It also doesn't mean that you can allow the tendencies associated with this form to just run rampant.

We all have relationships, for example. Some people might have the optimistic idea that after realization all relationship is going to flowing harmoniously. Great idea, isn't it! It doesn't make any difference. Just because there has been a realization of Consciousness being Consciousness doesn't mean that relationship in the day-to-day nitty gritty is going to be any better. Relationships function on honesty, commitment, and common sense. If you want a healthy relationship you need to be really honest, you need to be committed and present, and you need to be caring. These have nothing to do with being realized. You could have a completely unrealized person with a really flowing relationship because they know the principles through which relationship functions well. You could have a perfectly realized person with a terrible relationship.

The habits of the personality are always up for refinement, before realization and after realization. This is a common misunderstanding about non-dual teachings—the assumption that after realization everything just happens all on its own, or that we should just let things occur and not touch thought. What that means is that ninety-nine percent of the time one just allows dysfunction to continue. Why? The realization is that Consciousness is still and pure and perfect, but there is still a human being and there is still the possibility of choices—even though ultimately there is no choice. Be human. There's no problem. All this stuff is just common sense, and if one doesn't hold esoteric beliefs everything is very simple.

53

Natural Respect

*Y*ears ago I asked another teacher how to know when somebody is a true teacher. He replied that you should feel a natural respect and love for the teacher, and there should be laughter. All those things are completely present here, and I feel you are my true teacher.

I appreciate your respect, I really do. At the same time I want to make a confession, to honor your innocence. The laughter is a laughter we share. The respect is mutual and the love is mutual. I want you to know this, really deeply, because it's so important these days. Truly and honestly, we are all the same. I really mean it. I'm not just saying this to pass the buck.

I sit here because I was asked to. And I'll probably never know why. If there is any qualification, it is only that different bodies have different skills. Someone plays music, but if you gave me a guitar people would run away. Someone else cuts hair; you wouldn't want me to cut your hair. And someone else is a doctor, but you sure wouldn't want me dishing out pills. This body called Arjuna just came blessed with the gift of articulateness, that's all. This body has the capacity to put into words our mutual experience. But it's a mutual experience, and it feels very important to constantly emphasize this. I'm not a teacher. The meeting is the teacher. This gathering of friends is the teacher. I'm more like the facilitator of a teaching that is happening in the whole room.

At the same time, for whatever reason, I feel there are some of us who just pop open before the others, like popcorn. That's my sense of it.

I would advise you not to hold that idea. Anything is true if you believe it to be true. I would advise you not to look at it that way and I'll tell you why. Holding up an idea like that creates a

163

subtle form of separation. It also creates a foundation for post-ponement or waiting for something more. I guarantee you that if we took a weekend together to go camping or hiking, you would drop all notions like that. Everything you go through, I go through too. I'm just doing this because I was asked to and because the body has an articulateness. And perhaps also, to be fair, some capacity to hold presence. I had years of therapeutic training and that is a skill you learn—to stay present with people. But human beings are human beings. The whole gestalt changes when you stop pinning wakefulness onto a person and let it be everywhere. It's a radically different game we're in if we see it that way. There is truly no such thing as an enlightened person. It's a bogus idea. A person and enlightenment just don't go in the same sentence together. I'm not just playing around with semantics.

That is actually the very kernel of what is happening now on the planet. It's this pithy little point about hierarchical spiritual-ity, where the enlightened one is at the front and everyone else is trying to get it, or has partially gotten it, or kind of wobbling in it. In that theater there is only room for one in the auditorium to be seated at the front. It's the difference between that and the other side of the pivot, which is an ocean of awakening, planetary awakening. In this view everyone is That, and everyone in form has their little quirks. I know almost all the teachers personally who are teaching like I am, and I tell you, all of them go through stuff all the time. Some declare it outright and some hide it, that's all. I personally declare it. I like to have it all out on the table. We don't need to get into dirty laundry, but anything you could come up with, I could match you. Isaac Shapiro is another one; he is very honest. I'm not faulting either choice. Some teachers feel that to maintain the purity of the teaching, they should keep their private life private and maintain an appearance of purity.

I don't believe in that one.

Well, there is no need to believe or not believe it. It's just a choice of style.

To me, one of the greatest things Ram Dass did was to start showing me how human he was, years ago.

Jack Kornfield is the same. It's just a matter of personal style. These days I prostrate all limbs to the ground to someone willing to show up as ordinary and human. I'm very bored by enlightened gurus. It's just not interesting to me. But take a Jack Kornfield or a Ram Dass or a Stephen Levine—they are all willing to sit there and be real. When Stephen speaks of relationship with his wife, Ondrea, he doesn't say, "We've got the answer." He speaks of the churning and the deepening mercy in seeing what we all go through.

This is just how life works. There is nothing wrong with it. There are conditions that are not theoretically ideal. When those conditions arise it creates a little discomfort, and that discomfort starts a chain of creative impulse going which initiates creative action.

And the conditions may be ideal, even though one doesn't think so.

Yes, absolutely. Many of us carry the notion that all this shouldn't be happening. There should just be silence, just resting. To hold onto all of that is just a way of torturing yourself. Just let it be. Be human. Say you're in a relationship and the person leaves. If you don't feel something I would say you might want to get some psychiatric help.

This is a very interesting point because I was with another teacher for awhile and she said if you really feel something completely, it should be gone, just like that! I don't find that to be true.

Why should it be?

If there is major heartache or if there is tremendous catastrophe in your life, it is almost like birthing a baby—there is a gestation period where that has to...

How About Now?

If there is a pushing down of heartache or grief, that's not necessary and that can be liberated immediately. But it's natural for feelings to arise and fall. Just allow it all. We are human beings; if you want to know what it's like to be a human being, it's just what you're going through now. You can feel when there's a resistance to experience, and that can be liberated, but it doesn't mean the experience won't come again and again. It's natural, you see. If there's not enough money, it's natural that this will create first some contraction, out of the contraction some concern, and then concern will move into an impulse for action. The whole thing is so beautifully done. You put a seed in the ground and it sprouts and makes leaves. It continues to grow and become stronger until it becomes a tree. That's a miracle.

In the same way, if you cut your hand, you just apply a Band-Aid. You don't worry about it, and a few days later it's all healed up. That's a miracle. If you have a problem in your life, the chain of reactions that you go through that lead to resolution is a miracle. Just let it be. We're all the same—believe me. I've checked it out thoroughly.

(Laughter)

It's really a relief. We can let our hair down.

54

Only Now

If what is spoken of
Feels like something that is longed for
But not yet realized,
Then grasp it tonight!
Tonight!

There is no reason to postpone this.
It is available Now.
Only Now.
Now or not Now,
No tomorrow.

55

Your Own Truth

You already know all this,
But we play a little game.
You like to hear it said back to you.

It's not as much fun
Dialing your own wisdom hotline.

So you come to this place
And hire someone for the night
To tell you what you already know.

It sounds good
Because it's your own truth.

Sources

All of the chapters in this book were transcribed from live talks and dialogs. If you would like to order the audio or video tape that the chapter was taken from, here is a complete source list.

1   **The Antidote**
    Wednesday, October 21, 1998   *Laguna Hills, CA*

2   **The end of seeking**
    Friday, October 16, 1998   *Fairfield, IA*

3   **Value the Diamond**
    Sunday, November 8, 1998   *Nevada City, CA*

4   **Relaxing into That**
    Friday, July 3, 1998   *Jackson Hole, WY*

5   **Looking Beyond Changing Phenomena**
    Tuesday, March 31, 1998   *Marin County,CA*

6   **Awareness Itself**
    Thursday, January 14, 1999   *Nevada City, CA.*

7   **The Real**
    Friday, July 3, 1998   *Jackson Hole, WY.*

8   **Worship Only This**
    Tuesday, March 31, 1998   *Marin County, CA.*

9   **Relish Risk**
    Monday, February 23, 1998   *Los Angeles, CA.*

10 **The Window of Eternity**
    Friday, July 17, 1998   *New York NY*

11 **Cuckoo Banana**
    Tuesday, January 26, 1999   *Nevada City, CA.*

12 **Start at the End**
    Tuesday, April 7, 1998   *Marin County, CA.*

13 **The Clue**
    Tuesday, April 7, 1998   *Marin County, CA.*

14 **The Mutuality of Wakefulness**
    Tuesday, March 31, 1998   *Marin County, CA.*

15 **Relax Preference**
    Monday, July 6, 1998   *Marin County, CA.*

16 Give Up the Struggle
    Tuesday, March 31, 1998   *Marin County, CA.*

17 Marriage
    Monday, July 6, 1998   *Marin County, CA.*

18 Who Wants to be Enlightened?
    Tuesday, March 31, 1998   *Marin County, CA.*

19 Already Here
    Friday, July 17, 1998   *New York.NY*

20 No Preparation Required
    Friday, October 16, 1998   *Fairfield, IA.*

21 Wipe the Altar Clean
    Friday, June 26, 1998   *Denver, CO.*

22 A Natural Response to Life
    Tuesday, March 31, 1998   *Marin County, CA.*

23 Embrace Everything
    Friday, June 26, 1998   *Denver, CO*

24 Freedom from the Need to Be Free
    Tuesday, March 31, 1998   *Marin County, CA.*

25 What is in the Way of Finding?
    Tuesday, March 31, 1998   *Marin County, CA.*

26 The Individual is Doomed
    Thursday, October 22, 1998   *Laguna Hills, CA.*

27 The Wave is Already Wet
    Sunday, November 8, 1998   *Nevada City, CA.*

28 The Mind is a Trickster
    Tuesday, March 31, 1998   *Marin County, CA.*

29 Invisible Secret
    Thursday, December 17, 1998   *Nevada City, CA.*

30 Energy and Consciousness
    Tuesday, March 31, 1998   *Marin County, CA.*

31 Rest Here
    Tuesday, December 15, 1998   *Nevada City, CA.*

32 Drop In First
    Tuesday, April 7, 1998   *Marin County, CA.*

33 Listen to the Heart
    Tuesday, April 7, 1998   *Marin County, CA.*

34 It's Different Now
    Wednesday, July 1, 1998   *Jackson Hole, WI*

35 Nowhere to Go
    Friday, July 17, 1998   *New York.*

36 **In the Fire**
Friday, June 26, 1998   *Denver, CO.*

37 **Go Out and Boogie**
Tuesday, November 17, 1998 *Palo Alto, CA.*

38 **Let Go**
Thursday, May 7, 1998   *Los Angeles, CA.*

39 **We Meet as Beginners**
Monday, July 6, 1998   *Marin County, CA.*

40 **No Preferences**
Monday, July 6, 1998   *Marin County, CA.*

41 **Surrender**
Friday, July 3, 1998   *Jackson Hole, WY.*

42 **The Mirror**
Thursday, May 7, 1998   *Los Angeles.*

43 **Doubt is a Thought**
Wednesday, August 26, 1998 *Marin County, CA.*

44 **Contradictions are Embraced by the Heart**
Wednesday, July 1, 1998 *Jackson Hole, WI*

45 **Surrender All to the Divine Mother**
Monday, January 4, 1999 *Nevada City, CA.*

46 **The Birth of Love**
Thursday, July 23, 1998 *Washington DC*

47 **Embrace Pain**
Tuesday, February 2, 1999 *Nevada City, CA.*

48 **Seeds of Love**
Wednesday, July 1, 1998 *Jackson Hole, WI*

49 **Heartbreak**
Thursday, December 3, 1998 *Boulder, CO.*

50 **Welcome Everything**
Wednesday, June 24, 1998 *Denver, CO.*

51 **The Pull of the Heart**
Monday, November 16, 1998 *New York*

52 **Benefits**
Friday, December 4, 1998 *Boulder, CO.*

53 **Natural Respect**
Friday, December 4, 1998 *Boulder, CO.*

54 **Only Now**
Friday, June 26, 1998   *Denver, CO.*

55 **Your Own Truth**
Tuesday, March 31, 1998 *Marin County, CA.*

Thanks...

Many hands make a book happen.

I have no words available to express my gratitude and respect for Kate Bishop. Her dedication to this project, to her work and to the Truth extends way beyond the call of duty into the mysterious realms of true service.

Thanks to Norman Scrimshaw in Laguna Hills, who put aside his duties to the Southern California real estate market to get this book jump started,

Thanks to Illona Hanson, who became Rumi incarnate on many an evening and transformed my ramblings into much of the poetry you read here.

Thanks to Kamala Kadley, who dedicatedly transcribed way more material than we actually used, and always resurfaced asking for more.

Thanks to David Kisling, who sacrificed a number of trips to the Yuba river to slave over a hot keyboard to make the words fit in the page just right.

Thanks to Fred Keyser, Trisha Mitchell, Tony Kendrew, Marion Culhane, Vishwakarma, Jeremy Montz, Tomas Kuzara, Linda Savitz, and others for proofreading and spotting the typos. And thanks to Trisha for doing it all again.

Thanks to all our Satsang hosts in all the cities I visit, for creating the context in which the words could be spoken.

Thanks to the Nevada City sangha for being my true family.

Thanks to Rose Boyle for being Rose Boyle so perfectly and invisibly. Your support is beyond price.

And thanks to Abhi and Shuba for patiently bearing with a Dad who is always running off somewhere else on a airplane.

I love all of you.

—A—

About Arjuna

Arjuna has maintained an unbroken passion for spiritual awakening since 1971, and has lived and studied with teachers from a number of different traditions and backgrounds. In 1991 he met his true Teacher, H.W.L. Poonjaji, who pointed Arjuna's attention back to the immediate availability of the Self in this very moment. Arjuna lived with his Teacher for a year, and returned to the West to teach in 1992, at Poonjaji's request.

Arjuna conducts public Satsang throughout the US and Europe several times a week. He also meets with lovers of the eternal Truth for longer weekend intensives and retreats. With a group of dedicated friends he has developed the Living Essence Training, which prepares people to be facilitators of awakening with others.

Arjuna is the author of *Relaxing into Clear Seeing*, the *Living Essence Tapes Series*, and *The Wizard of Om*. He lives in Nevada City when he is not travelling, and is father to two sons.

About The Living Essence Foundation

The Living Essence Foundation is an non-profit church, in Nevada City, California.

We offer Satsang with Arjuna throughout the US and Europe, Satsang Intensives here at our facilities, as well as in a number of locations in the US and Europe.

To arrange for Arjuna to offer Satsang in your area, you can contact us at the address below.

We also offer a training program to prepare individuals to be facilitators of awakening.

For more information contact:

Living Essence Foundation
Box 2746,
Grass Valley, CA 95945
USA

phone: (530) 478-5985
or: 1-888-VASTNESS

fax: (530) 478-0641

e-mail: info@livingessence.com

Web address:
www.livingessence.com

Ordering Information

You can order more copies of this book, or other books and tapes by Arjuna.

From a bookstore:
Ask your local bookstore to order from Ingram, New Leaf or Bookpeople.

On the web:
Order online from amazon.com

By phone:
Call 1-888-VASTNESS.
Have your credit card ready.

By mail:
Send a check, money order or credit card number to:
Living Essence Foundation
Box 2746
Grass Valley CA 95945
USA

By fax:
Fax your order with a credit card number to:
1-530-478-0641

By e-mail:
E mail your order with a credit card number to:
orders@livingessence.com

Single copies cost $15.00 US
Shipping is $2.50 for the first book, and $1.50 for additional
    books.
California Residents add 7.375% tax ($1.11 per book).